Bevilacqua

christian meditations for young women

Anneke O. Hudson

Xulon
PRESS

Copyright © 2007 by Anneke O. Hudson

Bevilacqua
by Anneke O. Hudson

Printed in the United States of America

ISBN 978-1-60477-332-3

All rights reserved solely by the author. The author guarantees all contents are original and do not infringe upon the legal rights of any other person or work. No part of this book may be reproduced in any form without the permission of the author. The views expressed in this book are not necessarily those of the publisher.

Scripture taken from the HOLY BIBLE, NEW INTERNATIONAL VERSION®. Copyright © 1973, 1978, 1984 by International Bible Society. Used by permission of Zondervan Publishing House. All rights reserved.

The "NIV" and "New International Version" trademarks are registered in the United States Patent and Trademark Office by International Bible Society. Use of either trademark requires the permission of International Bible Society.

Scripture Quotations marked (NLT) are taken from the *HOLY BIBLE*, New Living Translation, copyright © 1996. Used by permission of Tyndale House Publishing, Inc., Wheaton, Illinois 60189. All rights reserved.

www.xulonpress.com

For Lydia…

This book was born when I first became a mother of a daughter.

May you always be thirsty for the Living Water.

Table of Contents

Special Thanks ix
What is Bevilacqua? 11
How to Bevilacqua 13
You are Expected to be Beautiful 15
Meditation 21
Cravings 25
At His Feet 29
Dance Like No One is Watching 33
Disgusting and Unaware 39
A Seasoned Sister 45
The Way 49
Contentment 55
Why Me? 59
Impossible Task (Jonah 1) 63
Nowhere He Won't Go (Jonah 2) 69
Disrobe (Jonah 3) 75
God's Perspective (Jonah 4) 81
Younique 87
Sex, Etc. Part One 93

Sex, Etc. Part Two 97
Sex, Etc. Part Three 103
Sex, Etc. Part Four 109
Sorrow or Guilt 113
Temptation 117
Renewed Commitments, Renewed Strength 123
Idols 129
Picture of a Woman of God 135
The Perfect Dad 141
One Thing 147
Still Standing 153
The Great Physician 159
Free to Be 165
Death Trap 171
Drop the Rocks 177
Set Apart 181
What Are They Thinking? 185
A Story About Grace 191
What For? 197
Thoughts on Today and Tomorrow 201

Special thanks...

To my loving husband Dan. You are more than I could dream up. I love you.

To my prayer sisters: Annamarie, Jessi, Joy and Sue. You have stood with me in prayer and encouraged me in writing this book for four years. I don't know what I would do without you.

To my sibs, Heidi, Kirsten and Aaron. You have filled my life with more depth, stories and laughter than a person deserves. I love you.

To my Mom and Dad—for trusting God enough to let me go on that first mission trip that set me on fire and for your patience, wisdom and generosity over the years. (I'm a parent now; I'm starting to 'get it'!)

To Kathi for the countless hours you have spent editing this book. You are more than a mother-in-law, you are a dear sister in Christ and a gift to me.

To all the women and a few men who have contributed to the wisdom in this book. I am sharpened and humbled.

To Amy, Hannah, Kim and Tayler, the "Bevilacqua Girls" who committed to test the manuscript. I have enjoyed being with you so much!

To Steve Smith for believing in this project and for offering experience, encouragement, and a gorgeous cover design.

To Aunt Reta for being the ultimate godmother. Thank you for your countless prayers and for showing me what it looks like to overflow with the things of God.

What is Bevilacqua?

∽

I have an artistic friend whose last name is Bevilacqua. Every time she pronounces it in her Italian accent, I am entranced by its poetic flow. I wish there were a little sound mechanism in the cover so that each time you open the book, you would hear her say, [bev ee lah´ kwa]. It is just that beautiful. What is even more inspiring is its meaning, 'drink water'.

I am reminded of a story in John 4 when Jesus came to a well in the middle of a hot day. A woman with a terrible past and reputation came to draw water. He lovingly defied religious and cultural taboos and talked with her. He knew everything about her, and cared enough about her to give her a new life worth living. He said,

> *"But those who drink the water I give will never be thirsty again. It becomes a fresh, bubbling spring within them, giving them eternal life."*
> *John 4:14 (NLT)*

> *She immediately replied, "Please, sir, ... give me this water! Then I'll never be thirsty again, and I won't have to come here to get water." John 4:15 (NLT)*

After being face to face with Jesus, He revealed to her that He was the Messiah. She left the well a completely different person. She even left her water jar sitting by the well so that she could run to town to tell the people that she had found something better. She had met the One who makes all the difference.

I suppose if the living water Christ referred to were actual water in the well, she would have lost no time and dived right in to '*bevilacqua*'.

We have a spiritual invitation to drink something better than this world has to offer. We can meet Jesus face to face in our desert and be filled with a fresh bubbling spring that will last to eternity. That is my reason for writing this book. Jesus filled me with His living water years ago and I have not been the same since. My hope is that in your youth, you will meet with Him daily and become a living spring, welling up with the beautiful things of God. Dive in, sister, and drink your fill.

How to Bevilacqua...

As you begin, you are welcome to work through each study in order or you may skip around to topics that are relevant for you at a particular time. Regardless of what order you choose, try to do one entry per day. If you are really thirsty, you may do additional journaling or explore more scripture through the "Overflowing" section. I encourage you to personalize this book by highlighting verses and making notes about struggles, frustrations, discoveries and answered prayer. You will experience amazing growth—not from my stories, but because there is power in prayer and in God's Word.

The more effort you put into the entries, the more you will get out of this book and your time with God. For example, if you are pouring out your heart to God and being honest with Him in the questions, there is no limit to what He can and will do, in and through you.

I encourage you to revisit lessons that you have completed and talk to God about what He has done and what else He may want to teach you through His Word. There are many opportunities to listen to what He wants to tell you—and there is nothing more exciting than the Most High God guiding, teaching and filling you so that you can know Him intimately and achieve the very purpose for which He created you. Will this happen in thirty days, sixty days, a year, ten years? I do not have that answer. In some ways, that is the most exciting thing about our God. He is more concerned that we are sitting face to face with Him than He is with religious obligation. I encourage you not to look for answers, but to look for Jesus and you will have more than you need for each day.

"Please, sir, ... give me this water! Then I'll never be thirsty again..." John 4:1 (NLT)

Real Wisdom from Real Women
 "Revelation 22:13 says, '*I am the Alpha and the Omega, the First and the Last, the Beginning and the End.*' Jesus is the beginning and the end and everything in between. That is Truth for my life, but it is also true for my days. I find when I start my day with Him in quiet time, and when I end my day with Him in quiet time, He takes care of everything in between. The lessons He teaches me in the morning are thoughts I can meditate on all during the day. But at night He does more than just wrap up my day for me. He starts preparing me for the next day. The words He speaks to me at night settle down in my heart and He instructs me while I sleep (Psalm 16:7). He was, He is, and He is to come. There is no better way to start and end my days than with the Alpha and the Omega." –Sue

May you be part of the unashamed minority.
May you join with other young women across the world to seek the face of Jesus.
May you rise before dawn to meet Him.
May you be intoxicated with His living water.
May your mouths be filled with laughter and your tongues with songs of joy. Psalm 126:2

Dear Jesus, thank You for another day to worship and serve You. Change my heart so that I may look less like me and more like You. Amen.

You Are Expected to be Beautiful

Explain your daily beauty routine: _____
_____
_____
_____
_____
_____

Roughly how much time do you spend getting ready in each of these categories?

    Shower: _____   Special Scents: _____
    Make-Up: _____   Hair Stuff: _____
    Outfit Selection: _____   Other: _____

Adding these up, about how much time does it take you to get ready before you leave your house on the average morning?
_____

Who are you motivated to impress with your beauty?
_____
_____

What is one part of your routine that you absolutely cannot miss before you start the day? _____
_____

As women, we have certain expectations of ourselves. We also feel the need to live up to the expectations of others. Do you feel the pressure? I remember one day sitting around the table with my sisters. I am the second of four children. One of my dad's long time friends stopped in on his way through town. As my dad introduced us, his friend responded, "You should keep having kids, because they keep getting prettier." He went on to explain that in another family the youngest daughter was the prettiest also.

Did you catch that? My little sister showed me up! As I sat there, I forced a smile and tried to be gracious, but in my heart I knew that I didn't measure up. I felt like I had disappointed my dad, his friend and myself. His words cut deeply. Being compared and evaluated like this throughout my school years made me believe that outer beauty defined who I was. Looking back, I now realize that I was seeking approval through others' opinions of my appearance. I could have spared myself a lot of pain had I ignored the voices of others and just listened to God's voice. Living in this perspective is a treasure few people seek after, but when uncovered, changes everything.

Do not misunderstand me. I am not trying to eliminate your beauty routine or encourage you to look like an unmade bed. Instead, the reason for this book is to help you discover your identity and purpose in your relationship with your Creator.

The Lord does not look at the things a man looks at. Man looks at the outward appearance, but the Lord looks at the heart. 1 Samuel 16:7

God does not see you as attractive as a result of your trying harder, doing more or scrutinizing yourself. Jesus wants to change us from the inside out. He provides the beauty. Not only that, but He longs for us to seek after Him so He can give us more than we could ever dream of.

I am not talking about having a phony Christian happiness. I am talking about spilling over with God's genuine love, joy and peace. You are unique and He created you for a special purpose. He wants to shape and bless you in every way. He loves you more than any person can or ever will and wants to do so much more in you.

My challenge for you from this point forward is to let God beautify you before you do your outer routine. Make your time with Him priority. That may require some sacrifice on your part. Do you need to set your alarm 20 minutes earlier? If you oversleep, are you willing to leave the house without finishing your outer beauty routine?

When you finish each study, meditate on the verse provided, highlight the phrases that really speak to you, copy it and keep it with you to read throughout the day. Then get your body ready to go. You will not regret having an encounter with Jesus before you begin each day. Psalm 5:3 says, *"In the morning, O Lord, you hear my voice; in the morning I lay my requests before you and wait in expectation."*

I pray that you shine the "extra something" that only God's Spirit can give. May you spill over with the gorgeous glow of Jesus today.

Thirsty?

I pray that from His glorious, unlimited resources He will empower you with inner strength through His Spirit. Then Christ will make His home in your hearts as you trust in Him. Your roots will grow down into God's love and keep you strong. And may you have the power to understand, as all God's people should, how wide, how long, how high, and how deep His love is. May you experience the love of Christ, though it is too great to understand fully. Then you will be made complete with all the fullness of life and power that comes from God. Ephesians 3:16-19 (NLT)

You should clothe yourselves instead with the beauty that comes from within, the unfading beauty of a gentle and quiet spirit, which is so precious to God. I Peter 3:4 (NLT)

May God give you more and more grace and peace as you grow in your knowledge of God and Jesus our Lord. By His divine power, God has given us everything we need for living a godly life. We have received all of this by coming to know Him, the One who called us to Himself by means of His marvelous glory and excellence. 2 Peter 1:2-3 (NLT)

What do you want to remember? Spend some time now talking with God about the things He revealed to you today.

Real Wisdom from Real Women
"Our value and self-worth come from being loved and accepted. God loves us and He accepts us but if we don't love Him or value Him, His opinion (or love) means nothing to us. Then, we look to the world for our value and worth. *We must first come to know Him, and then we can come to love Him.* Only then, will His love and acceptance for us become of value to us." –Joy

Overflowing
Psalm 139:1-18

Lord, change me by Your Word. Open my heart to take the time to let You speak to my whole being. Amen.

Meditation

Of all the ways I have grown in my faith over the years, meditating on scripture may be the most meaningful. We hear about many different cultures practicing meditation, but there is a profound difference between other faiths and Christianity. Other religions may seek to empty their minds through meditation, yet we look to *be filled by* God's Word.

In order to unwrap the gift of meditation, we must do our best to:

- Slow down
- Find a quiet place
- Let God open our minds to His voice and shut out distractions
- Be open to a change of heart as God directs us

When you have done these things, choose a scripture and let God speak to you through it. One way is to memorize and reflect on it again and again in your mind. You may also place more emphasis on certain words each time you say it. This allows you to grasp more fully and then soak up small portions of scripture. The goal is to allow the *word of Christ to richly live in us (Colossians 3:16).* In order to do this, we must read a text again and again, absorbing its richness and surrendering ourselves with its meaning. As you yield, the living Word of God will take on such life and power, you may not be able to put it into words. Your spirit will spill over as He does a mighty work in you.

Sometimes it is helpful to use your imagination. Read the verse or verses you select several times and imagine you are present. Perhaps you are in the crowd as Jesus teaches. In order to fully understand His mercy and grace, put yourself in the place of the crippled beggar or the prostitute. Allow yourself to hear his correction when He speaks to the self-righteous Pharisees. Stand before the foot of the cross when He gasps for breath and exclaims, *"Father forgive these people, because they don't know what they are doing." (Luke 23:34)*. Whatever the text, open your heart to it. It is one thing to read information; it is another to experience it. As Christ invites us to let His words remain in us, we must carefully take in His words and then let them take over.

Let's start with a short verse today. Allow yourself the time and quiet space to devote yourself to God's Word. In the verse below, Jesus is encouraging His followers not long before He is arrested and put to death...

Thirsty?

"I am leaving you with a gift—peace of mind and heart. And the peace I give is a gift the world cannot give. So don't be troubled or afraid." John 14:27 (NLT)

Write what you learned through this exercise. I encourage you to reflect on this verse the entire day or even the entire week. Let it take on meaning in your daily life, especially as you interact with others. Recall it again and again as you fall asleep at night. _____

_____
_____
_____
_____
_____
_____
_____

Challenge: Slow down and devote yourself to God's Word so that meditation becomes a well-developed habit when you study scripture.

Just a note...I wrote this entry a week ago and after writing it, decided to practice what I preached and meditate on a verse for a week. What I did not realize is that I was in an anxious state about really stupid things. I was carrying stress and passing it around to others. After meditating only a couple days, I realized that I had surrendered my anxious heart and need for control and let God be God in my life. I was full of His joy—the anxiety had left and I was laughing more and enjoying the simple things of life. Again, this is beyond total explanation. But I just had to thank God and you, my sisters in Christ for the opportunity! You have given me the privilege of teaching what I've learned...and the privilege of revisiting old lessons. God is keeping me spiritually fresh through this book!

Real Wisdom from Real Women

"I was at a servant event in south central India with five other girls and while we were there, we took part in worship experiences with Christian Indian youth. Americans and Indians took turns leading each night...the purpose was not only to worship but also to share our cultural differences while sharing our common Christian faith. One particular night, the leader of the Indian group (a young woman in her 20's who had been on many trips to the United States and served as our liaison) shared a meditation experience with us. She prepared us by saying that many people assume, incorrectly sometimes, that meditation is only for Middle Eastern religions. We were thick in Hindu country and had assumed the same. She explained that meditation was a cultural ritual, yet the Christians in India meditated as well. Meditation, she explained, was a way to empty before filling...and as Christians we were emptying ourselves from the cares of the world so that we could be filled with Christ. Meditation brings both clarity and filling. Obviously, people of other religions in her country were filling themselves with false gods. We allowed Christ to take over in us. It was a powerful discipline I learned from my Christian brothers and sisters across the world." –Jill

Overflowing
John 1 (Who is the Word? With whom are we filling ourselves?)
Colossians 3:15-17
John 15:5-17
Psalm 46:10 (A wonderful meditation verse)
Psalm 119:9-16

Lord Jesus, help me have Your desires as I live in this world. Amen.

Cravings

I am expecting our second child as I write. I can tell you a whole lot about cravings. Just the other day I decided I "needed" a s'more. I took a graham cracker from the diaper bag, a handful of mini marshmallows and hacked away at some Hershey kisses we had in a candy dish. Did you know that a toaster oven is pretty close to an in-home bonfire when it comes to making s'mores? At least *now*, while I'm pregnant, I have an excuse…but I have always had cravings. I come from a family who loves to cook and loves to eat and we do it very well. What do you crave in this life?

Chocolate	New clothes	A companion
Fried food	Attention	Acceptance
More $	Affection	Pizza
Good friends	Approval	Physical touch

Other cravings unique to you:

What does this scripture say to you about craving? As you read, underline phrases that speak to you.

Do not love this world nor the things it offers you, for when you love the world, you do not have the love of the Father in you. For the world offers only a craving for physical pleasure, a craving for everything we see, and pride in our achievements and possessions. These are not from the Father, but are from this world. And this world is fading away, along with everything that people crave. But anyone who does what pleases God will live forever. 1 John 2:15-17(NLT)

There is not one person living on this earth that cannot help but feel convicted by this scripture at some point in their lives, if not on a daily basis. Scripture does tell us that there is something we *should* crave. What is it? _____

_____

Like newborn babies, you must crave pure spiritual milk so that you will grow into a full experience of salvation. Cry out for this nourishment… I Peter 2:2 (NLT)

If we crave things that do not last more than we crave spiritual things of Christ, there is hope. We can ask that He transform us so that we desire things that are best for us. How does the above passage tell us to ask? _____

_____

Go ahead and cry out to God for gifts that will last forever.

Thirsty?

Take a look at how God promises to answer us when we ask Him for spiritual things in order to experience Him more fully:

Jesus replied, "I am the bread of life. No one who comes to me will ever be hungry again. Those who believe in me will never thirst." John 6:35 (NLT)

[Jesus said] "The Spirit gives life; the flesh counts for nothing. The words I have spoken to you are spirit and they are life." John 6:63

[Jesus said] "Ask and it will be given to you; seek and you will find; knock and the door will be opened to you. For everyone who asks receives; he who seeks finds; and to him who knocks, the door will be opened. Which of you, if his son asks for bread, will give him a stone? Or if he asks for a fish, will give him a snake?" Matthew 7:7-10

You will seek me and find me when you seek me with all your heart. Jeremiah 29:13

Those who know your name trust in you, for you, Lord, have never abandoned anyone who searches for you. Psalms 9:10 (NLT)

Blessed are those who hunger and thirst for righteousness, for they will be filled. Matthew 5:6

When we ask God to help us crave Him, He will! Look for it. Ask Him to help you get up in the morning to seek His face. Ask Him to help you remember what you've learned from scripture. Ask Him to help you obey Him. Ask Him for an extra measure of His love and a clear picture of how much He loves you. Ask, ask, ask! He will always say, "YES" to these requests because it is what He desires of us.

Look for ways to feed your spirit's cravings as God answers your prayer. As you notice the changes over time, write them below with the corresponding date. Take notice that as you really begin to let God's words live in you, the things of this world that once seemed like such a big deal will fade to the background and you will see clearly the things of God. What a privilege!

My spiritual craving /
Today's Date   **His Answer / Date**

Challenge: Try giving up an earthly love that you have for one week. For example, if you decide to give up TV, secular music, shopping or chocolate, quietly say a prayer each time you pass on an opportunity; offer it to God as worship and ask Him to fill you to overflowing with His love, patience, wisdom, self-control, discernment and humility... See Galatians 5:16-26

Real Wisdom from Real Women
  "How freeing it was for me to finally surrender and call on the Lord to change my **desires**. Tired and disillusioned from longing for change and struggling to achieve it in my own strength, I finally realized that the situation may remain the same but only God is able to change the genuine and sincere desires of my heart." –Joy

Overflowing
Romans 8:11-16
1 Peter 4:1-6
Isaiah 55

Dear Jesus, I love You. Thank You for giving me this time with You. Help me to hear Your voice. Amen.

At His Feet

~~~~

I've got to hand it to you; you are devoting another day to your King. It is a sacrifice a lot of people are not willing to make. I commend you. The best part is that my words of praise will soon mean nothing compared to being in the presence of your Savior. You may not be completely put together on the outside, but the Most High God, Creator of the Universe is at work in you and will have graced your day.

What thoughts, worries, or burdens have taken over your mind and heart today? We all have something. Part of making God priority is to let Him reign over everything - *especially* those things that race through your mind and heart. So what is it that is heavy on your heart? _____

_____
_____
_____
_____
_____
_____

We do not need to spend our time here on earth worried or bothered by things in this life. Philippians 4:6 says, *"Do not be anxious about anything, but in everything, by prayer and petition, with thanksgiving, present your requests to God."*

I invite you to try something that may seem a little radical. Trust me. Close your door or find a spot where you won't be distracted or interrupted. Lie on the floor—face down. (I understand this may seem very strange if you've never prayed this way before, but allow Jesus to teach you a new way to be with Him.) Imagine Jesus is physically present with you. Lay all those burdens at the feet of Jesus and make Him King of your day; talk to Him. He is there with you. It is all right to stay there as long as you need to—until you have truly laid your burdens before Him. Can you hear Jesus? He asks you to…

"Come to me, all of you who are weary and carry heavy burdens, and I will give you rest. Take my yoke upon you. Let me teach you, because I am humble and gentle, and you will find rest for your souls. For my yoke fits perfectly, and the burden I give you is light." Matthew 11:28-30 (NLT)

Face Time—At His Feet

Now that you have unloaded your burdens, fill yourself with His words, His peace, His wisdom:

Thirsty?

"I have told you all this so that in me you may have peace. In this world you will have trouble. But take heart! I have overcome the world." John 16:33

I keep asking that the God of our Lord Jesus Christ, the glorious Father, may give you the Spirit of wisdom and revelation, so that you may know Him better. I pray also that the eyes of your heart may be enlightened in order that you may know the hope to which He has called you, the riches of His glorious inheritance in the saints, and His incomparably great power for us who believe. Ephesians 1:17-19

Highlight the portions that are especially meaningful to you. Take a minute to memorize one of the passages.

Many times we pray and give our burdens to God and then we take them right back and carry them with us throughout the day. Each time you are tempted to pick up the burden again, remember to leave it exactly where it should stay: at the feet of Jesus.

Real Wisdom From Real Women
"If someone offers to help you with chores around the house or some difficult task, would you let them help you? You would be crazy not to! We should be just as willing to let Jesus carry our burdens—He wants to, that's why He came." –Jessi

Have a wonderful day. Keep His words close to your heart.

Overflowing
Isaiah 40:11, 28-31

Great God, set me free so that I can praise You with all that I am. Unlock in me whatever may be holding me back from giving You the praise You deserve. Amen.

Dance Like No One is Watching

It was a warm, summer evening. The windows to the mansion (where we lived and worked in exchange for rent) were open and all the lights were on. Dan was finishing a paper for a seminary class and I was waiting up for him in my summer jammies. The music playing was so beautiful, I just couldn't help myself. I started to dance using ballet moves and spinning about on the hardwood floor. I never took ballet, but I imitated whatever I had seen by waving my arms and twirling. You see, I *thought* no one was watching me. Just as I tried another cool, made-up move with my arms, I glanced out the window to see the owner of the mansion looking up into our window as he walked to their front door. Instead of playing it cool and pretending not to notice—pretending that I really knew what I was doing, I instinctively screamed and ran out of the room. Smooth...

I was embarrassed because I had let down my guard in the presence of someone else. For a brief moment in my twenties, I was four and full of life. We are friends with the owners and have since laughed about my silliness. Yet, the thought has crossed my mind more than once—*What if it wouldn't have mattered?* What if the only one I cared about in life was my Creator? What if I let Him lead me in my dancing and singing? What if as I lived, I lived for an audience of One? What if honoring Him freely and joyfully became a life of worship, an offering of praise?

The apostle Paul got to a place in his ministry where he only lived to please God. Read his words carefully:

Obviously, I'm not trying to be a people pleaser! No, I am trying to please God. If I were still trying to please people, I would not be Christ's servant. Galatians 1:10

Let's discover what our lives can be like when we seek to please Christ only, specifically, as we develop an active worship life. Scripture gives examples of certain physical postures we may use: clapping, lying face down, raising our hands, kneeling, dancing and bowing our heads. God intends for us to honor Him so freely, that our hearts spill over and we do not hold back physically from giving Him praise. God reveals a beautiful example of this in His Word. Read about a passionate worshipper in scripture:

Thirsty?

Then King David was told, "The LORD has blessed Obed-edom's household and everything he has because of the Ark of God." So David went there and brought the Ark of God from the house of Obed-edom to the City of David with a great celebration. After the men who were carrying the Ark of the LORD had gone six steps, David sacrificed a bull and a fattened calf. And **David danced before the LORD with all his might**, *wearing a priestly garment. So David and all the people of Israel brought up the Ark of the LORD with shouts of joy and the blowing of rams' horns.*

But as the Ark of the LORD entered the City of David, Michal, the daughter of Saul, looked down from her window. When she saw King David leaping and dancing before the LORD, *she was filled with contempt for him.*

They brought the Ark of the LORD *and set it in its place inside the special tent David had prepared for it. And David sacrificed burnt offerings and peace offerings to the* LORD. *When he had finished his sacrifices, David blessed the people in the name of the* LORD *of Heaven's Armies. Then he gave to every Israelite man and woman in the crowd a loaf of bread, a cake of dates, and a cake of raisins. Then all the people returned to their homes.*

When David returned home to bless his own family, Michal, the daughter of Saul, came out to meet him. She said in disgust, "How distinguished the king of Israel looked today, shamelessly exposing himself to the servant girls like any vulgar person might do!"

David retorted to Michal, "I was dancing before the LORD, *who chose me above your father and all his family! He appointed me as the leader of Israel, the people of the* LORD, *so I celebrate before the* LORD. **Yes, and I am willing to look even more foolish than this, even to be humiliated in my own eyes!** *But those servant girls you mentioned will indeed think I am distinguished!" 2 Samuel 6:12-22 (NLT, bold added)*

How about you? Are you willing to feel a little foolish, yet step out of your comfort zone to offer God praise? The first thing I constantly want to remember is to be open to God's leading. Worship is about adoring our Creator and Savior, not entertaining our own needs or insecurities. Ask Him to set your spirit free. Enjoy His presence. The more you practice worshiping on your own time, the more meaningful it will be when you are with your church family.

Here are some examples of what worship may look like for you. Try them out over the next few weeks. Feel free to look up the corresponding scriptures to inspire you.

Attitude ~Let your whole being praise God throughout the day in your thoughts, actions and how you interact with others. Romans 12:1-2; Psalm 100:2; John 4:24; Psalm 51:17

Body ~
Mouth-Sing or tell God how great He is. Write from the depths of your soul who God is to you personally. Seek out time to sing or talk to Him out loud when you are alone. (The car is a great place!) By the way, if you don't have a great voice, don't hold back. Your Creator made you the way you are—give Him your best and sing away!

Face Down-Forget yourself by laying face down and being completely humbled by His greatness. Revelation 19:1-10

Kneel-Let this be a way you come before Him in humility and honor. Psalm 95:6; Ephesians 3:14; Luke 22:41; Acts 21:5

Clap-Find some worship music and adore Him with your hands. Psalm 47:1; 98:8

Bow Head-Worshipping in quiet stillness is extremely powerful. 2 Chronicles 29:30; Psalm 95:6; Matthew 28:90

May God continue to lead us closer to Him as we live free lives of worship! Enjoy living as though He is the only one watching you.

Real Wisdom from Real Women
"One of my favorite things to do is to watch my children dance around the house when worship music is playing. They are so free and fun to be with. They don't care what they are wearing, if they are wearing anything at all! They make up new moves and dance until they are exhausted. They teach me how to worship with all that I am." –Anonymous

Overflowing
Colossians 3:16
Philippians 2:5-11
Psalm 93 and 104

Lord Jesus, You are the Purifier. Cleanse me from the things I am ashamed of and forgive me for the sins I'm not even aware of. I need You, Jesus. Amen.

Disgusting and Unaware

When I was a kid growing up on a farm in southern Illinois, much of my time was spent outside getting dirty. One particularly hot summer, some family friends from the city came to visit. City folk seem to be both curious and repulsed by farm-life pastimes and so it was with this brother/sister pair. For a reason still unknown to me, we decided to make a mudslide in the ditch on our property. We found a spot in the ditch that was especially mushy which made our jumping, sliding and rolling particularly fun. It was not long before we were covered from head to toe in mud. This was not a problem for us because we were having such a great time; however, the mud smelled uniquely foul. When we returned to the house our parents were horrified to discover that the part of the ditch we chose to play in was the part where the sewer drained. That's correct, ladies. We were playing in sewage. Before we were even allowed into the house for a shower, our parents hosed us off.

It is interesting to me that all of the fun we were having seemed a lot less fun when we realized what we had been doing. A seemingly harmless mudslide was more like a toxic pit. I'm sure you can imagine that the only thing we wanted at that point was a good shower and clean clothes.

Suppose we went about our day without a shower. Can you picture our slimy little bodies snuggling under the covers for a good night's sleep?

Identify a time when you have been so filthy that you could do nothing but head to the shower. _____

_____
_____
_____
_____
_____

There are so many spiritual lessons we can learn from my disgusting episode. To a perfect God, our sin reeks worse than sewage. He longs to make us clean. In fact, that's the very reason that Jesus gave His life on the cross. He came to cleanse us before we even knew we were in the sewer of sin.

Have you been going about your days spiritually filthy? What sin(s) are covering you? It might be obvious that something you are doing is hurting yourself and God, or you may be unaware. If you are not sure, take some time to ask God to open your eyes to sin that He wants to cleanse you from. Use the space below to write what He reveals to you. _____

_____
_____
_____
_____
_____
_____
_____
_____
_____

How ridiculous would it have been if my parents had pointed out that I had played in the sewer and I decided to ignore them, or worse yet, would have reacted in a hostile way, refusing to bathe?

How do we hurt ourselves when we ignore God's desire to cleanse us? _____
_____
_____

How do we hurt Him? _____
_____
_____

Thirsty?
Take a look at David's experience with sin in Psalm 32.

O what joy for those whose rebellion is forgiven, whose sin is put out of sight! Yes, what joy for those whose record the Lord has cleared of sin, whose lives are lived in complete honesty!

When I refused to confess my sin, I was weak and miserable, and I groaned all day long. Day and night your hand of discipline was heavy on me. My strength evaporated like water in the summer heat.

Finally, I confessed all my sins to you and stopped trying to hide them. I said to myself, "I will confess my rebellion to the Lord." And you forgave me! All my guilt is gone.

Therefore, let the godly confess their rebellion to you while there is time, that they may not drown in the floodwaters of judgment. For you are my hiding place; you protect me from trouble. You surround me with songs of victory. (NLT)

How did David feel when he held on to his sin? _____
_____
_____

What happened when he came clean? _____
_____
_____

What does God surround us with when He rescues us from the toxic pit of sin? _____
_____
_____

When God forgives, the sin is gone. He does not hold our sin against us when we come to Him and He is not going to remind you of your sin at a later date. David said, "all my guilt is gone." That means He not only washes away our sin, but He even wipes away that horrible guilty feeling that builds up. We are free to walk in His grace. Let it flow over you today like water so that you can dance in His songs of victory.

You may have people remind you of something you have done in the past, but your Savior is not like that. Remember that once you confess it, God forgets it. Hold His words close to your heart. If you have trouble forgiving yourself, continue to meditate on the scripture verses and ask God to change your perspective.

Scripture to treasure throughout your day:

I waited patiently for the Lord; He turned to me and heard my cry. He lifted me out of the slimy pit, out of the mud and mire; He set my feet on a rock and gave me a firm place to stand. He put a new song in my mouth, a hymn of praise to our God. Many will see and fear and put their trust in the Lord. Psalm 40:1-3

Real Wisdom from Real Women
"There have been many times in my life when a song or a memory reminds me of past sin. I am tempted to feel that overwhelming sense of guilt again but then I realize that if I continue to wallow in the guilt after Christ has forgiven me, I have discounted His grace. It is like throwing the cross in His face." -anonymous

Overflowing
2 Corinthians 5:17
Psalm 103:12
Romans 5

Lord Jesus, You know my needs before I even ask. Send an amazing person into my life that will lead me closer to You. Amen.

A Seasoned Sister

Almost everyone who knows me well, knows about my Aunt Reta. Aunt Reta is a woman who believes in the power of prayer and has countless stories about how God has answered prayer over the years. I am especially blessed because she was the "godmother" my parents chose when I was born. I know that every day she gets up before anyone else in her home and prays for me while she sips her coffee. In fact, this very day as you are reading this, I am confident that Aunt Reta will have prayed for me. I realize that this is an especially rare gift. Not everyone has an Aunt Reta, but God places people in our lives to encourage and bless us—mature Christians who cheer us on in our walk of faith.

Before we go any further, I want you to know that you have been in my prayers before the very first entry was ever written. I may not know your name, but our Almighty God does, and I am convinced that He is doing an exceptional work in you. I believe that His desire is for you to grow with someone who has known Him a very long time. I would like you to take a second to clear your mind. Ahhh....that feels nice. Now, think of mature Christian women who you know are walking with Christ. Ask God to bring to mind women who exhibit: authenticity, compassion, confidentiality, wisdom and a fruitful prayer and devotional life. (You will know because they will have that "God glow" that surpasses outside appearances.) Think about older women in your church who possess the characteristics seen in Galatians 5, then meditate upon the beauty that the Holy Spirit provides when He is alive and active in a person's life.

Thirsty?

But when the Holy Spirit controls our lives, He will produce this kind of fruit in us: love, joy, peace, patience, kindness, goodness, faithfulness, gentleness, and self-control. Here there is no conflict with the law. Those who belong to Christ Jesus have nailed the passions and desires of their sinful nature to His cross and crucified them there. If we are living now by the Holy Spirit, let us follow the Holy Spirit's leading in every part of our lives. Galatians 5:23-25 (NLT)

List three to five people that came to mind as you meditated.

_____

_____

_____

Now, take a look at your list and ask God to select the woman that would be especially helpful to you at this time. Circle her name and make a point to ask her if she will be your spiritual mentor who prays for you on a regular basis. You may even brainstorm with her about how you can grow from her experiences with Jesus. Then, read the verse below. This is one example of how she can pray for you.

So we have continued praying for you ever since we first heard about you. We ask God to give you a complete understanding of what He wants to do in your lives, and we ask Him to make you wise with spiritual wisdom. Then the way you live will always honor and please the Lord, and you will continually do good, kind things for others. All the while, you will learn to know God better and better. We also pray that you will be strengthened with His glorious power so that you will have all the patience and endurance you need. May you be filled with joy, always thanking the Father, who has enabled you to share the inheritance that belongs to God's holy people, who live in the light. Colossians 1:9-13 (NLT)

Read the verse again, but this time, use it to pray for yourself. When you have finished, use the space below to write a prayer for your seasoned sister. _____
_____
_____
_____
_____
_____

Real Wisdom from Real Women
"God never denies me what I need. If He does not supply it through a parent or family member, He gives me wonderful people who bless me with more than I need." —Barb

Overflowing
Get a glimpse of a fabulous mentor relationship by reading Paul's letters to young Timothy.
1 Timothy 1
1 Timothy 4:11-16

Jesus, priceless treasure; be near me and fill me. Open my eyes to Your truth. Help me to speak truth and love freely so that all those around me will encounter You. Amen.

The Way

As you read the verses below, highlight the portions that reveal who Jesus is and the reason He came.

Thirsty?

Jesus shouted to the crowds, "If you trust me, you are really trusting God who sent me. For when you see me, you are seeing the one who sent me. I have come as a light to shine in this dark world, so that all who put their trust in me will no longer remain in the darkness." John 12:44-46 (NLT)

...so he explained it to them. "I assure you, I am the gate for the sheep," he said. "All others who came before me were thieves and robbers. But the true sheep did not listen to them. Yes, I am the gate. Those who come in through me will be saved. Wherever they go, they will find green pastures. The thief's purpose is to steal and kill and destroy. My purpose is to give life in all its fullness." John 10:7-10 (NLT)

For Jesus is the one referred to in the Scriptures, where it says, "The stone that you builders rejected has now become the cornerstone." There is salvation in no one else! There is no other name in all of heaven for people to call on to save them. Acts 4:12 (NLT)

And this is the way to have eternal life—to know you, the only true God, and Jesus Christ, the one you sent to earth. John 17:3 (NLT)

Jesus told him, "I am the way, the truth, and the life. No one can come to the Father except through me." John 14:6 (NLT)

What surprises you about these passages? _____
_____
_____
_____

What does Jesus tell us about His purpose for coming to earth? _____
_____
_____
_____

What do you believe? _____
_____
_____
_____

    I had a defining moment with my very best friend when I was 17 years old. She and I grew up together and we talked about everything. We laughed really hard – a lot; so much, in fact, that I stopped wearing mascara because I knew I would end up looking like a raccoon by the end of the day. I cannot tell you how much I loved and still love this friend. Her opinion meant the world to me.
    One summer I returned from a short-term mission trip and told her stories about how hard our team worked to bring the gospel to the broken-hearted in Ukraine. I was high on God and so excited about the way He used me and my team.

Of course, I had to share my joy with my dear friend. As I did, she told me she had also done some searching over the summer and came to the realization that she just could not come to terms with Jesus being the only way to heaven. "How can a devout Buddhist not go to heaven?" "What about people who have never heard about Jesus?" She had taken questions like these to her minister while I was overseas. To my complete shock, the words her minister told her changed her heart and our friendship forever.

Her minister shared that Jesus is a great way for some, but not for all. Surely a devout Buddhist would still go to heaven even if he rejected Jesus! I sat stunned. What could I say? I wrestled with how to answer her questions. I explored the issue for myself. I didn't know what to do – all of a sudden things were different between us.

I suspect that you have had similar situations or that you are struggling with some of the same questions. If so, talk to Jesus about them. No human can convince or argue anyone into the truth. You need an encounter with Jesus to know this truth; and to know Him, you have to submit to Him and receive Him as your Lord.

Take a minute to talk to Him about this right now. Feel free to journal any questions you may have. _____
_____
_____
_____
_____
_____
_____
_____
_____
_____

May I share a few scripture passages with you that have been a tremendous help to me?

...for He wants everyone to be saved and to understand the truth. For there is only one God and one Mediator who can reconcile God and people. He is the man Christ Jesus. I Timothy 2:4-5 (NLT)

You can enter God's Kingdom only through the narrow gate. The highway to hell is broad, and its gate is wide for the many who choose the easy way. Matthew 7:13 (NLT)

You will seek me and find me when you seek me with all your heart. Jeremiah 29:13

He went on a little farther and fell face down on the ground, praying, "My Father! If it is possible, let this cup of suffering be taken away from me. Yet I want your will, not mine." Matthew 26:39 (NLT) NOTE: Jesus prayed this prayer before He gave His life for all people. Why would He have hung on the cross to die if there were millions of other ways to get to heaven?

Consider this question: For an unbeliever, who is doing the rejecting? Is it God or that person? _____
_____

Throughout your life, you will find (and probably already have) that this is not a popular belief. It sounds harsh. It sounds exclusive. Sometimes you may even experience hostility from people who have not yet been changed by the power of Christ's love. The one thing I wish I would have thought to share with my friend is that Jesus died for every single person who has ever walked the face of the earth. There is nothing exclusive about it. He willingly gave His life for all people, spanning all history. Color, race, paycheck, social status, intelligence, rule-keeping and tight-rope walking have absolutely no effect on your qualification for God's grace. He came for all – period.

I am praying for you. I am praying that God will fill you with the perfect balance of His love and patience - that all may know He is the only way to true life by His love and grace at work in you. Drink it up, sister. He wants to use you to reveal Him to the world.

Challenge: Make this passage your everyday motto. Pray it in the morning as you face each day.

Instead, you must worship Christ as Lord of your life. And if you are asked about your Christian hope, always be ready to explain it. But you must do this in a gentle and respectful way. Keep your conscience clear. Then if people speak evil against you, they will be ashamed when they see what a good life you live because you belong to Christ. 1 Peter 3:15-16 (NLT)

Love is patient…1 Corinthians 13:4

Real Wisdom from Real Women
   "I have a family member who does not believe in Jesus. And I'm loving 'the hell' out of him." -Marlene

Overflowing
If this issue is troubling for you, meditate and pray Mark 9:24: *"I do believe, but help me not to doubt." (NLT)*
John 1 (The whole chapter is great.)
2 Corinthians 4:3-11

Dear Jesus, help me to really understand the joy of living in whatever circumstance You have given me. Amen.

Contentment

I grew up with very few needs. Truly, I cannot name one physical need I had that was not met as a child. I remember desperately *wanting* a Cabbage Patch Kid and a pair of Reeboks like my friend, Charady. Overall, though, my family was blessed materially. Not rich, but blessed. Funny how so many of my grade-school years were clouded with fierce jealousy over a pair of shoes and a doll—especially now that the shoes are out-dated and the fact that I saw an old Cabbage Patch at a garage sale recently—not a pretty sight. It's even more interesting to me that the time I truly understood blessing and contentment was when I was in a third world country for a month: Cold showers, washing every bit of laundry by hand, uncomfortable beds, tons of insects, warm water for refreshment and long days of ministry in 80 degree heat. Was it because I met brothers and sisters who had far less than me and spilled over with generosity and gratitude because they knew Jesus? Was it because I *needed* to experience the joy of Christ with less? Whatever the means, I know that our Lord graciously began to let me see the world through His eyes. I finally started to understand what Paul was talking about in Philippians 4:11-13:

I am not saying this because I am in need, for I have learned to be content whatever the circumstances. I know what it is to be in need, and I know what it is to have plenty. I have learned the secret of being content in any and every situation, whether well fed or hungry, whether living in plenty or in want. I can do everything through Him who gives me strength.

Can you think of a time when you were in absolute need? How did God meet it? Did He meet it differently than you expected? _____

_____
_____
_____
_____
_____

Are you *wanting* anything at this point in your life? Write about it. _____

_____
_____
_____

Is there something that is robbing you of contentment in Jesus? (Maybe your sights are set a little higher than a Cabbage Patch Kid.) In other words, do you find yourself thinking, "When I have such and such or when so and so asks me out…, then I will be happy." Or, do you find yourself thinking that others who have more than you must have a much better life? For example, a billionaire has no real needs or reason to complain. Often, we will experience some kind of earthly struggle, so that our dear Lord can teach us a much more valuable spiritual lesson.

True contentment is, "Lord, if my situation never changes, I am okay with that because You are in control." In a sense, it is absolute surrender of wants or needs because we trust that our loving Provider will meet any need we have in His perfect timing and in His own way. True contentment is knowing inner peace even when everything around us is in chaos. Only Jesus can enable us to know peace regardless of our life story.

Thirsty?
Psalm 23 expresses contentment so beautifully:

The LORD is my shepherd; I have everything I need.
He lets me rest in green meadows; He leads me beside peaceful streams.
He renews my strength.
He guides me along right paths, bringing honor to his name.
Even when I walk through the dark valley of death,
I will not be afraid, for you are close beside me.
Your rod and your staff protect and comfort me.
You prepare a feast for me in the presence of my enemies.
You welcome me as a guest, anointing my head with oil.
My cup overflows with blessings.
Surely your goodness and unfailing love will pursue me all the days of my life, and I will live in the house of the LORD forever. (NLT)

Are there any phrases that jumped out at you? What words of comfort did you receive? _____
_____
_____
_____
_____
_____
_____
_____
_____

Feel free to mark the verses and write notes alongside portions that blessed you. For example, make a note of a dark valley you've been in or list blessings He's given you that are overflowing. (When I take time to list what I have, my discontentment fades.)

Challenge: As you find yourself thinking that you will be happier or that life will be easier when...., take that thought captive and recall a phrase from one of the two scriptures we've looked at. Ask God to unlock the secret of contentment that He revealed to Paul. Ask Him to give you peace and joy in your situation. It's one of those requests He will never deny. He longs to give you His peace in this crazy, mixed up world. It's also a reminder that our hopes and dreams are to be perfectly filled in a completely different home called heaven. Until we meet there someday, God's peace to you, sister.

Real Wisdom from Real Women
"It's only money." — Aunt Reta

"When I recognize and confess my own discontentment, I see a glimpse of how gracious my Father really is. I see that I am so rich in Him. He blesses me with things I don't often recognize as blessings. When I long for more of other things, He still blesses me and doesn't remove His hand of blessing because of my sin. He loves me inspite of myself. He knew there would be times I would feel Jesus wasn't enough. Yet, He gave Him to me anyway. What love! That is the love that makes us content." –Jessi

Overflowing
Psalm 4:8
John 14:27; John 16:33 (Jesus' words)
Colossians 3:12-17 (* verse15)

God, reveal to me Your purpose in my relationships. More than that, let me see the reason You have called me to serve. Amen.

Why Me?

~~~

I recently heard about a pastor in Asia who was persecuted for his faith. He had been thrown in prison dozens of times. A pastor from the United States asked him what prison was like—if he hated going there. To that, he replied, "Oh, no. God gives us so many opportunities when we are imprisoned. We are able to share the gospel freely because He opens doors for us to do so." He went on to tell about how the forced labor in the rice paddies is the perfect time to share openly about Jesus Christ. He was grateful for wherever God led him because he knew, no matter how difficult, it was an honor to bring the message of Christ and salvation. He was allowed to be a messenger of the Most High God and that was enough for him.

Why does God trust us with His work? Read the following scripture carefully.

Thirsty?

And so, since God in His mercy has given us this wonderful ministry, we never give up. We reject all shameful and underhanded methods. We do not try to trick anyone, and we do not distort the word of God. We tell the truth before God, and all who are honest know that. 2 Corinthians 4:1-2 (NLT)

Read verse one again. What is the reason we have been put in ministry? _____

_____

As a result of our God's mercy, what will we never do?

_____

_____

What is our "code" as His ministers?
1. To reject _____
2. We do not _____
3. We do not _____
4. We tell _____

In one of my college classes we were asked to write our own mission statements. One well-meaning person wrote, "To get people to heaven in any way possible." As we analyzed the statement, another classmate joked, "We baptize them and then shoot them." She made a good point: We minister out of obedience to God, not just for the end result.

We serve a holy God who calls us to simply love and obey Him in honesty and integrity. That may mean being misunderstood. It may also mean rejection, discomfort and awkwardness. For some it may even mean beatings, imprisonment and death. Yet, we do not give up. Paul, a man who knew persecution well, wrote these words:

No, in all these things we are more than conquerors through Him who loved us. For I am convinced that neither death nor life, neither angels nor demons, neither the present nor the future, nor any powers, neither height nor depth, nor anything else in all creation, will be able to separate us from the love of God that is in Christ Jesus our Lord. Romans 8:37-39

Consider these questions and talk to the Lord about them.

What wonderful ministry has He given you in this season of your life? (Remember, it may not seem so wonderful on the surface. Paul wrote 1 and 2 Corinthians. As you read some of the suggested passages within them, you will learn that the "wonderful ministry" he referred to included rejection, stoning, flogging, and imprisonment. See 2 Corinthians 6:3-10) _____

_____
_____
_____

When are you most tempted to give up? _____

_____
_____
_____

How has God encouraged you in your ministry today?

_____
_____
_____

Why me? Why you? Because our Lord Jesus is so rich in mercy, He included us in His mission long ago. (See Ephesians 2:10)

Real Wisdom from Real Women
"I've been reassured, time and time again, by the knowledge that the Bible and Christ's words are promises to me. They are not merely words or stories, but they are promises.

If I can remember that when I'm lonely, afraid, confused or searching for answers, I am so much more at peace." —Joy

Overflowing
Ephesians 2:4-10
John 17:20-26 (Did you know that Jesus prayed for us before His death?)
2 Corinthians 4

Great God, help me to hear and believe Your message. Speak directly to my heart. Amen.

Impossible Task

Thirsty?

¹The LORD gave this message to Jonah son of Amittai: ² *"Get up and go to the great city of Nineveh! Announce my judgment against it because I have seen how wicked its people are."*

³*But Jonah got up and went in the opposite direction in order to get away from the LORD. He went down to the seacoast, to the port of Joppa, where he found a ship leaving for Tarshish. He bought a ticket and went on board, hoping that by going away to the west he could escape from the LORD.*

⁴*But as the ship was sailing along, suddenly the LORD flung a powerful wind over the sea, causing a violent storm that threatened to send them to the bottom.* ⁵*Fearing for their lives, the desperate sailors shouted to their gods for help and threw the cargo overboard to lighten the ship. And all this time Jonah was sound asleep down in the hold.* ⁶*So the captain went down after him.* "*How can you sleep at a time like this?*" *he shouted.* "*Get up and pray to your god! Maybe he will have mercy on us and spare our lives.*"

⁷*Then the crew cast lots to see which of them had offended the gods and caused the terrible storm. When they did this,*

Jonah lost the toss. [8]"What have you done to bring this awful storm down on us?" they demanded. "Who are you? What is your line of work? What country are you from? What is your nationality?"

[9]And Jonah answered, "I am a Hebrew, and I worship the LORD, the God of heaven, who made the sea and the land." [10]Then he told them that he was running away from the LORD.

The sailors were terrified when they heard this. "Oh, why did you do it?" they groaned. [11]And since the storm was getting worse all the time, they asked him, "What should we do to you to stop this storm?"

[12]"Throw me into the sea," Jonah said, "and it will become calm again. For I know that this terrible storm is all my fault."

[13]Instead, the sailors tried even harder to row the boat ashore. But the stormy sea was too violent for them, and they couldn't make it. [14]Then they cried out to the LORD, Jonah's God.

"O LORD," they pleaded, "don't make us die for this man's sin. And don't hold us responsible for his death, because it isn't our fault. O LORD, you have sent this storm upon him for your own good reasons."

[15]Then the sailors picked Jonah up and threw him into the raging sea, and the storm stopped at once! [16]The sailors were awestruck by the LORD's great power, and they offered him a sacrifice and vowed to serve him.

[17]Now the LORD had arranged for a great fish to swallow Jonah. And Jonah was inside the fish for three days and three nights. Jonah 1 (NLT)

What did God ask Jonah to do? _____

_____
_____
_____
_____

Let's really dive into this passage. Insert your name in the blank:

Get up, _____, leave your comfortable surroundings—your safe life and go to a hostile city in the Middle East. Tell them that I, your God, will destroy them for their lifestyles.

Would you respond any differently than Jonah? I can tell you that the first words out of my mouth would probably not be, *"Yes, Lord. Thank you for speaking so clearly to me and giving me such and important purpose and mission. I am so honored to be your messenger."*

I would probably logically argue that I had made it up: *certainly God would not ask me to do such a thing.*

What does Jonah do after God reveals His mission?
_____
_____

Zoom in on verses 7-10. Let's break apart what is taking place: The sailors are freaking out because of the terrible storm. They believe they are going to die and beg their gods for help. It becomes obvious to them when they throw dice that this storm is a result of something that has to do with Jonah. They ask, "Who **are** you?" Jonah answers, "I worship the all-powerful Creator who made me and everything and I decided to run away from Him."

That makes me laugh. Jonah doesn't look too bright at this point. He physically runs from God, who created and controls and knows all things. After I laugh, though, I realize how similar I am to Jonah. We most likely have not physically run from God; but how have we run from Him in our minds, hearts and spirits? Is there any impossible task that you face? Are you running from abilities or missions that your Creator has given you? Ask Him to convict you of something you have been ignoring or "running from." Journal here.

_____
_____
_____
_____
_____
_____

The things He has called me to do look more impossible than running away from God. How preposterous is that? Let's look at what is possible with God:

Jesus looked at them and said, *"With man this is impossible, but with God all things are possible."* Matthew 19:26

For it is God who works in you to will and to act according to his good purpose. Philippians 2:13

...so it is with My word that goes out from My mouth: It will not return to me empty, but will accomplish what I desire and achieve the purpose for which I sent it. Isaiah 55:11

What characteristics of God appear to be present in the scripture passage from Jonah?

>Merciful   Wrathful   Fair   Powerful
>All-Knowing

I see all of these characteristics, however, God's mercy seems to be most prevalent. It was God's mercy that caused Him to pursue us and use us. Only a god who doesn't care would leave us to follow our own selfish desires. God loved Jonah, the sailors, and the people of Nineveh enough to display his power. List at least 5 ways God revealed Himself in this passage:

1. _____

2. _____

3. _____

4. _____

5. _____

God loves you and those He wants to reach through you enough to pursue you. Don't run away from Him, run to Him and let Him do the seemingly impossible through you.

Talk to Him about what He's asked you to do, large or small. Raise your hands in surrender and receive the tasks He's given you. He will reveal little or huge missions to you throughout your day and your life. Look for them. Welcome them. The seemingly little things can have more impact than we can even trace. The seemingly huge task may cut our egos down to size and make room for more of God's mercy and grace to spill out of us. Raise your hands in surrender. May we lovingly offer the words of Mary to the one who knows us best: *"I am the Lord's servant... May it be to me as you have said."* Luke 1:38

Use these words as your prayer today. Take any of the scripture from this lesson, copy it and meditate on it.

_____
_____
_____
_____
_____
_____
_____
_____
_____
_____

Real Wisdom from Real Women

"It was like the Holy Spirit was screaming at me telling me to pray with him. My mind kept trying to reason me out of it, giving me thoughts like...*it will be so awkward, surely he will hate the idea, I will look so ridiculous even suggesting it, he just isn't 'there' in his faith*...and then I finally obeyed. I asked my husband if he wanted me to pray for him. He looked at me with grateful eyes and said, 'yes'. That was the first time we prayed like that together. It took us to a new dimension in our relationship." —Sue

Overflowing
Luke 1

Lord Jesus, what do You want to teach me from this crazy story? Open my heart. I trust You. Amen.

Nowhere He Won't Go

I will never forget a powerful lesson that God taught me on my first mission trip. I was privileged to learn it in a place I had never been. When I was sixteen, I spent one month in Nicaragua. It was the longest I had ever been away from home. I had a room to myself in what used to be a home for nuns. The old convent stood on top of a small mountain that overlooked Managua. It was beautiful. I remember feeling so close to God. I would lie on the creaky old cot and see the stars through the window—wondering why I wasn't afraid or lonely. I believe it was because in the solitude and in a place with no phone, no family and little familiarity, I felt at home because God was there. At times I would wake from a deep sleep and feel called to pray for our ministry in the city. There, in the darkness, I was home. I knew that no matter where He would call me in my life, I could never be out of His reach.

Thirsty?

¹Then Jonah prayed to the LORD his God from inside the fish. ²He said, "I cried out to the LORD in my great trouble, and he answered me. I called to you from the world of the dead, and LORD, you heard me! ³You threw me into the ocean depths, and I sank down to the heart of the sea. I was buried beneath your wild and stormy waves. ⁴Then I said, 'O

LORD, you have driven me from your presence. How will I ever again see your holy Temple?'

[5] "I sank beneath the waves, and death was very near. The waters closed in around me, and seaweed wrapped itself around my head. [6] I sank down to the very roots of the mountains. I was locked out of life and imprisoned in the land of the dead. But you, O LORD my God, have snatched me from the yawning jaws of death!

[7] "When I had lost all hope, I turned my thoughts once more to the LORD. And my earnest prayer went out to you in your holy Temple. [8] Those who worship false gods turn their backs on all God's mercies. [9] But I will offer sacrifices to you with songs of praise, and I will fulfill all my vows. For my salvation comes from the LORD alone."

[10] Then the LORD ordered the fish to spit up Jonah on the beach, and it did. Jonah 2 (NLT)

From Jonah's perspective, he was out of God's presence and far from God's reach. We have a hard time imagining what it must have been like in the belly of a fish. In fact, there are probably a lot of people who would chalk this up as a Biblical fairy tale. Friend, do you believe this is so much more than a story? This story really happened. There really was a man named Jonah who ran from God's call and was burped up on a beach. I am so happy to believe it, because God speaks to me and tells me that there is no place on earth He cannot be for me, with me and behind me.

Think of a place you have been that you thought God could not be. It doesn't matter if it is a spiritual or physical place. Have you been in utter despair, family chaos, tangled in sin or far away from those you love? Write about that experience.

_____
_____
_____
_____
_____
_____
_____
_____

King David knew God well. Read what he wrote in Psalm 139:1-12:

[1] O LORD, you have searched me and you know me.
[2] You know when I sit and when I rise; you perceive my thoughts from afar.
[3] You discern my going out and my lying down; you are familiar with all my ways.
[4] Before a word is on my tongue you know it completely, O LORD.
[5] You hem me in-behind and before; you have laid your hand upon me.
[6] Such knowledge is too wonderful for me, too lofty for me to attain.
[7] Where can I go from your Spirit? Where can I flee from your presence?
[8] If I go up to the heavens, you are there; if I make my bed in the depths, you are there.
[9] If I rise on the wings of the dawn, if I settle on the far side of the sea, [10] even there your hand will guide me, your right hand will hold me fast.

11 If I say, "Surely the darkness will hide me and the light become night around me," 12 even the darkness will not be dark to you; the night will shine like the day, for darkness is as light to you.

The Bible is very clear about what happens when we call to the God of the Universe for help. (See Jonah 2:2 from earlier in this study) He knows exactly where we are and what we need. Where are you? There is no place that He cannot go. Remember, He died and went to the depths of hell so that you and I would not.

Memorize a verse or two from Psalm 139 (above) and reflect on God's closeness to you as you go about your day.

Real Wisdom from Real Women
"I was in the car alone when the tears came. It all seemed so unfair. Here it was, New Year's Eve. My husband and I should have been planning a romantic evening—just the two of us—to welcome in the New Year. Instead, we were planning a divorce. At this very moment, the betrayal, the lies, the ugly words, the destroyed dream of our future together were just too much. I had tried so hard to keep all the pain locked away deep in my heart, but the sobs came unbidden. Even though I was alone, I was still angry with myself for losing control over these feelings.

"It was then that I felt God enfolding me in His embrace and His words filling the car, 'Go ahead and cry, my daughter. Let it all out. Grieve the broken dreams, then let them go. I have so much planned for you this New Year! Dreams that you have never dared even imagine! More joy than you can contain! Trust in me. I will never leave you. I will never divorce you.'

"And He held me there in the car and I cried.

"God keeps His promises. He is mending the pieces of my broken heart as quickly as I will allow Him. Some days, I insist on doing the stitching myself, leaving huge gaping holes, but God replaces them with finely spaced, tiny ones that mend those broken pieces so seamlessly. When He is finished, they will be barely evident." –Susan

Overflowing
Psalm 46 and 91
Jeremiah 33:3

Lord, help me to be broken before You so that I may experience Your mercy and know Your heart for me. Amen.

Disrobe

I will never forget a time the man of my dreams came to visit on summer break of college. He decided to make it a surprise. Only my parents knew he planned to leave at 5:00 a.m. to make the six-hour trip to see me. I had decided I was going to paint the fence that lined the pasture around our home. It was such a dreaded job that my parents paid us when we were desperate for money. I got up early to beat the summer heat and dressed in the absolute worst clothes I could find. (The paint is like thick tar and it will ruin clothing. Also, to clean it off your skin, you have to use gasoline and then take a long shower to be rid of the scent. Thus, the reason for my ensemble.) Are you ready for this? I found a pair of old cut off sweats that were a little snug so my belly bulged over the top a bit. I wore an old stretched out sports bra under a work shirt and pathetically out of date, cheap running shoes. I couldn't find anything to hold my hair in place and I was already behind schedule, so I grabbed some clothespins to keep my hair out of my face. Classy, eh? About the time I was heading out to the fence, I saw Dan drive up looking wonderful in his brother's sporty Camero. Was it a surprise! Times like this can really test our vanity, ladies. I failed this test. Instead of running to see him and being excited about the surprise, I ran like a maniac into the house tearing clothespins out of my hair and ripping the old clothes off. I wouldn't have minded old jammies, but this getup was just too much for me to handle. We laughed pretty hard when I explained what state I was in, but what a disappointment for him to see his beloved running away from him! How disappointing that I couldn't trust his love when I was at my outward worst. I have since found that you trust those you love the most with your worst appearance and inward vulnerability.

Thirsty?

Jonah 3: Jonah Goes to Nineveh

[1]Then the LORD spoke to Jonah a second time: [2]"Get up and go to the great city of Nineveh, and deliver the message of judgment I have given you."
[3]This time Jonah obeyed the LORD's command and went to Nineveh, a city so large that it took three days to see it all. [4]On the day Jonah entered the city, he shouted to the crowds: "Forty days from now Nineveh will be destroyed!"
[5]The people of Nineveh believed God's message, and from the greatest to the least, they decided to go without food and wear sackcloth to show their sorrow.
[6]When the king of Nineveh heard what Jonah was saying, he stepped down from his throne and took off his royal robes. He dressed himself in sackcloth and sat on a heap of ashes.
[7]Then the king and his nobles sent this decree throughout the city: "No one, not even the animals, may eat or drink anything at all. [8]Everyone is required to wear sackcloth and pray earnestly to God. Everyone must turn from their evil ways and stop all their violence. [9]Who can tell? Perhaps even yet God will have pity on us and hold back his fierce anger from destroying us."
[10]When God saw that they had put a stop to their evil ways, he had mercy on them and didn't carry out the destruction he had threatened.

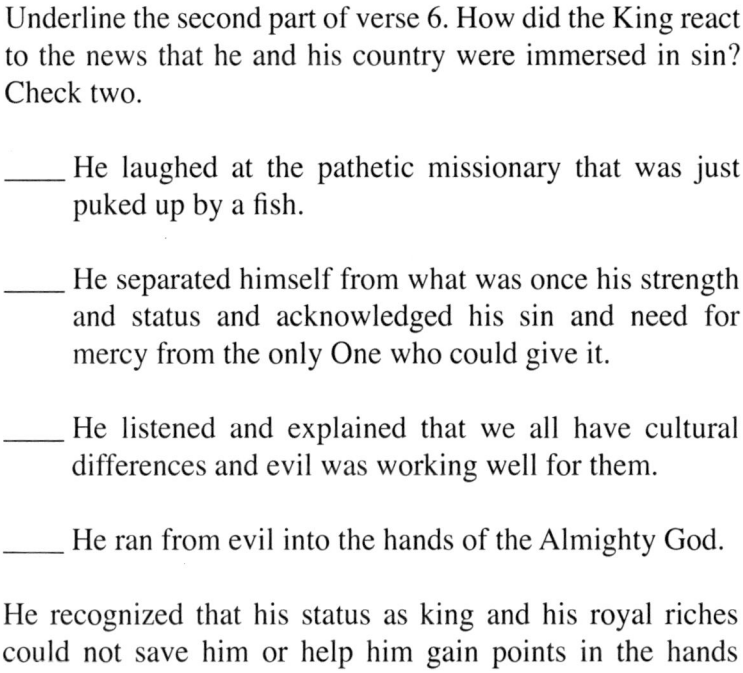

Underline the second part of verse 6. How did the King react to the news that he and his country were immersed in sin? Check two.

____ He laughed at the pathetic missionary that was just puked up by a fish.

____ He separated himself from what was once his strength and status and acknowledged his sin and need for mercy from the only One who could give it.

____ He listened and explained that we all have cultural differences and evil was working well for them.

____ He ran from evil into the hands of the Almighty God.

He recognized that his status as king and his royal riches could not save him or help him gain points in the hands of the holy God. The only thing he could do, was humble himself to receive the mercy of Jonah's God. He let God and the entire city see him as a vulnerable, helpless human being. God showed His unfailing love once again and changed the heart of an entire nation.

Have you disrobed enough to let your Beloved see every part of you? Talk to Him about evil thoughts, desires and ambitions that could destroy you. What will you shed today?

Make sure He sees the parts that you're most ashamed of so that He can surprise you with life changes more wonderful than you can imagine. Have you let Him see you at your worst? How has He spoken to your heart today? Write to Him about that in the space below.

_____
_____
_____
_____
_____
_____
_____
_____
_____

Real Wisdom from Real Women

"As I sit here to type my 'wisdom' I am a little teary-eyed. Teary because I just read the story above and my heart sank thinking about how merciful God is. What does mercy really mean? In a word, compassion. You see, as I started to write I thought, 'God, how long has it been since I exposed myself to you?' My heart ratted me out and replied, 'Jami, it has been too long.'

"I volunteer on most Sundays at a church of about 3,000 that has a number of buildings and facilities. My job is to welcome visitors, show them where to go, and hopefully let them see the Light of the World shining through me. I have a toothy smile, friendly demeanor, and I am fairly confident that my outward appearance is that of 'a good' Christian (Christians sometimes tend to hide behind our holy face even when things are crumbling around us and we need God and other Christians the most). In a church that big it is easy to hide from pastoral staff and even friends.

"This past week I failed to spend much time with God. I was even very distracted during worship on Sunday. You know, looking around, singing with no feeling. Perhaps I also failed to mention to God that I was sorry about last week when in frustration a few bad words slipped out of my mouth. The sermon was about faith. I didn't take the time to explain to Him that I have been struggling with the faith to trust Him fully and give up things in my life that are stumbling blocks. I have been afraid that if I give those things up, I might not get what I want in the timeframe that I want it. So I hang on to what is comfortable instead.

"So some of you are still thinking, that's nothing compared to my life. Well, here's a doosie, I became pregnant before I got married. I am telling you that it is the WRONG way to go about things. There are consequences for sin and there have been times of real struggle because of my actions.

"There is a point, though. I remember that at the time I was terrified to tell my parents. They are Christians. I was a Christian. I met my boyfriend at a *church retreat*. For about two months I had morning sickness. Do you know that when I confessed to my mom that I was pregnant the morning sickness went away immediately? As soon as I exposed the truth the fear was gone and I was no longer sick. She didn't even react the way I thought she would, instead she showed me mercy. Because God is merciful, "We know that in all things God works for the good of those who love him, who have been called according to his purpose." (Romans 8:28). He took my act of sin and still gave me a wonderful child who reminds me of the abundant love of Jesus.

"I believe the only way to be free from sin is to acknowledge it before God. His mercy and compassion is what makes us want to change. Jonah was hiding from God's will not long before he went to Ninevah. It was God's compassion that gave him a second chance to fulfill his calling and be obedient. The King and the people of Ninevah acknowledged their sin. God showed them mercy because of their repentance and did not destroy the city like Sodom and Gomorrah.

"Don't wait to invite God in to your life, even if that means He will see your imperfections. Like He doesn't already know they are there?! Don't run from Him when you sin or because you have already sinned. Instead, talk to Him before you think of taking a drink, have a chat in the middle of that kiss that could potentially go too far, tell Him how you are hurting after you have blown it full-on and have hit rock bottom. If you can do that, He will help you. If you fail to talk to Him until it is too late, don't be scared. Get back to Him as soon as you think about it. Don't be afraid to expose yourself before God. He loves you unconditionally and He won't reject you— ever." — Jami

Overflowing
Psalm 51
Isaiah 57:15-21
Isaiah 66:2

Dear Jesus, give me Your eyes for my own life and for those around me. Amen.

God's Perspective

~~~

Thirsty?

¹This change of plans upset Jonah, and he became very angry. ²So he complained to the LORD about it: "Didn't I say before I left home that you would do this, LORD? That is why I ran away to Tarshish! I knew that you were a gracious and compassionate God, slow to get angry and filled with unfailing love. I knew how easily you could cancel your plans for destroying these people. ³Just kill me now, LORD! I'd rather be dead than alive because nothing I predicted is going to happen."
⁴The LORD replied, "Is it right for you to be angry about this?"
⁵Then Jonah went out to the east side of the city and made a shelter to sit under as he waited to see if anything would happen to the city. ⁶And the LORD God arranged for a leafy plant to grow there, and soon it spread its broad leaves over Jonah's head, shading him from the sun. This eased some of his discomfort, and Jonah was very grateful for the plant.
⁷But God also prepared a worm! The next morning at dawn the worm ate through the stem of the plant, so that it soon died and withered away. ⁸And as the sun grew hot, God sent a scorching east wind to blow on Jonah. The sun beat down on his head until he grew faint and wished to die. "Death is certainly better than this!" he exclaimed.

⁹Then God said to Jonah, "Is it right for you to be angry because the plant died?"
"Yes," Jonah retorted, "even angry enough to die!"
¹⁰Then the LORD said, "You feel sorry about the plant, though you did nothing to put it there. And a plant is only, at best, short lived. ¹¹But Nineveh has more than 120,000 people living in spiritual darkness, not to mention all the animals. Shouldn't I feel sorry for such a great city?"
Jonah 4

Revenge is sweet to our human hearts, is it not? We ourselves love to be shown mercy, but it is so tough to see others receive it when they're clearly in the wrong. Our God has an entirely different perspective. He *delights* in showing mercy. Do you know why that is? For one thing, it's His very nature. He not only knows the destruction that awaits us without His mercy: a life of hell on earth and then endless torment for all eternity; but He also knows our potential when we've been transformed by His mercy. He is the beginning and the end. He sees us beyond the realm of time and knows what great plans He has for us. To be transformed by His mercy, no matter how wretched we are, makes all the difference.

There is a true story about a woman who had been seeking God faithfully by meditating on scripture and devoting time in prayer. One day as she was walking to her car in the parking lot, a serial rapist and murderer put his gun to her back and told her to get in the car. As he proceeded to give her instructions, she told him to shut his mouth because she was going to pray for him! She spent the next several hours explaining God's unconditional love to this horrid man. She knew God's mercy so well that she could look into the eyes of a cold-blooded killer and show him grace. By the end of the day, he had emptied his bullets into her purse, confessed his sins to Jesus and received His grace. Not only that, but he turned himself into the authorities and years later was executed by lethal injection. It is said that he went to the death chamber with a confession of Christ on his lips. We will someday meet this man—no longer a murderer, but a saint who no more deserved God's grace than you and I.

She could have freaked out or shook her finger at him and rattled off the ways he had angered God, but, you see, Grace Himself was at work in her and in this man. She was able to convey mercy because she recognized her need for it. Not only that, she had been receiving a fresh look at God's grace in her daily life. She had not become calloused to what a merciful God He is.

Jonah had a little trouble seeing ministry from God's perspective as we all do sometimes. How would *you* respond to his complaints? _____
_____
_____
_____

How did God respond to Jonah? _____
_____
_____
_____

To whom is God leading you to show mercy today? _____
_____
_____
_____
_____

If you are having a tough time being gracious (as I sometimes do), spend some time meditating on the grace God has shown to you in the **"Overflowing"** scriptures. Write a thank you prayer to God for ways that He shows you His great mercy and unconditional love. _____

_____
_____
_____
_____
_____
_____
_____

Real Wisdom from Real Women

"Why is it so hard to be gracious towards others who have wronged us or who we feel don't deserve grace? I've struggled with that question for quite a while. I was hurt by some people who I feel should have known better. Like Jonah, I would prefer to run away from them rather than work with them. I would rather see them pay for what they did rather than see them comfortable with what they did; and that is exactly how Satan wants me to react. He doesn't want Grace or Mercy to get in the way of getting even, carrying a load of bitterness in your heart, or just being downright ungracious to those who have hurt us. Being gracious is something I thought I was good at until this incident happened. Then I realized that the only one good at being gracious is the One who gives us Grace, and that is Jesus, Jesus, only Jesus. Was He not gracious and merciful to me when I lashed out at someone who didn't deserve it? Was His Grace and Mercy not covering me when I was in the pit of despair, crying, angry, bitter, worried, and lacking in faith? He could have just as easily left me on my own, like Jonah wanted Him to do with Nineveh, but He chose not to. He chose to cover me with a king-sized blanket in His Grace and Mercy and He's asking me to remember that when I meet those who hurt me. Paul closes many of his Epistle's with these beautiful words:

"The grace of the Lord Jesus Christ be with you." That grace is what makes us forgiven Christians. I want Grace and Mercy to be a banner I carry each day so others can see that I'm not running away . . . I'm staying in the Nineveh that God has called me to, sheltered under the umbrella of His Grace and Mercy, and letting others share that shelter with me." — K.

Overflowing
Micah 6:8
Psalm 103
Psalm 116
Romans 3: 10-27
Romans 5:6-11

Lord, help me to surrender the things I'm doing that You have not called me to do. Help me to spend my time using the gifts You gave me. I don't want to wish for other people's gifts. Help me to know what You've called me to do in each stage of my life. I'm listening. Amen.

Younique

I went to a very small elementary school and I have good memories overall, but the thing I regret the most is trying so hard to be athletic when it was obviously not my thing. Since it was *the* thing to be good at sports, I gave it my best shot. God used those attempts to build character, but I will tell you that when I quit volleyball in the eighth grade, it was incredibly freeing. My first clue should have been that I could barely get the ball over the net for a serve — in fifth through eighth grade. I could feel everyone holding their breath when it was my turn to serve. I had a lot of encouragement, but very little ability. The reason I joined the team every year was because the other three girls in my class were in volleyball and I didn't want to be the only one not playing. Through the years, I've tried to pay close attention to the phrase that I believe God has placed in my head and heart: *But Anneke, you were the only one created to be you. There are things you are wonderful at. Run after those things.*

Is there anything that you are doing right now that is not "you"? What is it? _____
_____
_____
_____

Have you compared yourself to others wishing that you had some feature, gift or ability that is unique to them? In what way(s)? _____
_____
_____
_____

Isaiah 45:9-10 may convict us of times that we have not accepted His creation in us:

Destruction is certain for those who argue with their Creator. Does a clay pot ever argue with its maker? Does the clay dispute with the one who shapes it, saying, "Stop, you are doing it wrong!" Does the pot exclaim, "How clumsy can you be!" How terrible it would be if a newborn baby said to its father and mother, "Why was I born?" "Why did you make me this way?" (NLT)

Take some time to confess those desires to your Creator.

Isaiah 64:8-9:
And yet, Lord, you are our Father. We are the clay, and You are the potter. We are all formed by Your hand. Oh don't be so angry with us, Lord. Please don't remember our sins forever. Look at us, we pray, and see that we are all Your people. (NLT)

Let Him speak words of forgiveness to you.

Psalm 103:11-12:
For as high as the heavens are above the earth, so great is His love for those who fear Him; as far as the east is from the west, so far has He removed our transgressions from us. As a father has compassion on His children, so the Lord has compassion on those who fear Him.

There is no one like you in all the world. Does that excite you or scare you? You may feel a little of both. First of all, take a deep breath. There's no competition to be you. You no longer have to be or do something else. With that comes responsibility. Take a look at God's conversation with Jeremiah:

Thirsty?

⁵"I knew you before I formed you in your mother's womb. Before you were born I set you apart and appointed you as my spokesman to the world."
⁶"O Sovereign LORD," I said, "I can't speak for You! I'm too young!"
⁷"Don't say that," the LORD replied, "for you must go wherever I send you and say whatever I tell you. ⁸And don't be afraid of the people, for I will be with you and take care of you. I, the LORD, have spoken!"
⁹Then the LORD touched my mouth and said, "See, I have put my words in your mouth! ¹⁰Today I appoint you to stand up against nations and kingdoms. You are to uproot some and tear them down, to destroy and overthrow them. You are to build others up and plant them." Jeremiah 1:5-10 (NLT)

Write down every encouraging thing that God says to His frightened young kid: _____
_____
_____
_____
_____

Did you notice something else in that scripture? What does God do for Jeremiah? (v.9) _____
_____
_____
_____

You'll notice as you study scripture and as you experience God at work in your life, that whenever He commands us to do something He also provides the means for us to fulfill that command.

One example of this is when He says, *"Be perfect as your Heavenly Father is perfect." Matthew 5:48*

Who did He provide to take our place in our far-from-perfect state? _____
_____

In the passage from Jeremiah, He tells Jeremiah to speak and gives him the very words he is to say! Remember that God has called you to do something unique in every season of your life. No matter what that looks like—no matter how huge or insignificant it may seem—keep in mind that your Creator will provide everything you need to serve Him. He will lovingly guide and take care of you as you seek to follow Him.

God has called you to do something in your generation that no one else can. The only way to figure that out is to get to know Him and as He reveals spiritual truth and opportunities to you—follow them.

How does He sometimes reveal our gifts to us? First of all, pay attention to what people compliment you on—the compliments that reflect *you*, not your appearance. (By the way, honor your Creator by accepting them, not denying or brushing them off.) Compliments are not always an indicator of what you are called to do, but pay attention.

Listen to what you love. What makes you get up early and stay up late? What do you find yourself dreaming about? Is there something you are really passionate about?

Commit these promises of God to memory and journal to Him about them. Let Him speak to your soul and move you to do exactly what you were created for one day at a time.

Take delight in the Lord, and He will give you your heart's desires. Commit everything you do to the Lord. Trust Him, and He will help you. He will make your innocence as clear as the dawn, and the justice of your cause will shine like the noonday sun. Be still in the presence of the Lord, and wait patiently for Him to act. Psalm 37:4-7 (NLT)

For God is working in you, giving you the desire and power to do what pleases Him. Philippians 2:13 (NLT)

Now glory be to God! By His mighty power at work within us, He is able to accomplish infinitely more than we would ever dare to ask or hope. May He be given glory in the church and in Christ Jesus forever and ever through endless ages. Amen. Ephesians 3:20 (NLT)

Challenge: Try to avoid doing things that are not you. It may be a school activity, hobby or anything that drains your energy and takes you away from your passions. Look for ways to spend time with God, who knows you best, and follow the path He has for you. Encourage a friend. Recognize God's unique creation in someone else and let him or her know you see the Lord at work.

Real Wisdom from Real Women
"Follow your gifts. I used to think, 'Oh I wish I could sing or do what they do...', but that isn't what I was called to do. Now, I wake up at night or early in the morning thinking about a certain person and I wonder, 'Why did they pop in my head?' Then I know. I was called to pray for them!"
—Aunt Reta

Overflowing
Proverbs 16:1-9

God, help me to welcome Your teaching in this area of my life. Open my heart to Your perfect love for me. I want to know the truth. Amen.

Sex, Etc. Part One

Consider these statements. Are there any you have thought or said?
- How far can I go without having sex?
- At least I'm ½ a virgin.
- I will not kiss until I'm married.
- The Bible doesn't say anything about oral sex.
- It's alright to have sex as long as your life plans aren't affected.
- My friends talk about their experiences all the time. Is there something wrong with me?
- I plan to date, but I won't have sex.
- I want to have sex, I just don't want to get pregnant.
- I have only kissed guys and I don't want it to go any further.
- Technically, you can fool around and have sex after you're engaged.
- I want to marry a virgin.
- I have given so much away. I am so ashamed.
- I don't think there are any strong Christian men out there, so I have to settle for less.
- Even though I'm a virgin, I like to at least know that guys want to have sex with me.
- I will only allow a guy to court me.

- I'm waiting for the right guy and then, who knows?
- It's okay to have sex with the person I'm going to marry.
- I've made out with other girls.
- I'm a virgin except for my mouth.

You could probably write your name or someone you know by most of these statements. First of all, I want to caution you to not condemn anyone, including yourself for thinking or saying these things. We live in a world that has sent us a lot of lies. We can remain self-righteously pure or we can wallow in guilt. Neither of these is the answer. Let's look to Jesus and His Word for truth and grace. In this series, we will explore what He tells us.

Next, I need to ask you, do you *really* want to know what the Bible says about purity? We're going to pick apart some scripture and ask ourselves some tough questions. Do you truly give all of your desires, hopes, dreams, mistakes, and all of your thoughts to Jesus? Be honest with Him as you write to Him about your attitudes and desires. Ask Him to speak directly to you. Ask Him to make your heart ready so that He can teach you.

Thirsty?

Meditate on and pray Psalm 51:6 and write your honest thoughts to God.

"But you desire honesty from the heart, so you can teach me to be wise in my inmost being." (NLT)

Take time to listen...What truths did He speak to your heart as you prayed? _____

_____
_____
_____
_____
_____
_____
_____

Real Wisdom from Real Women

"I ordered 'Ultimate Love Songs' from Time Life. Sounds kind of silly, I know, but there are some really good songs on there. I was listening to them this weekend and it brought back lots of memories of my youth, dating and such. I was reminded again of how unhealthy that part of my life was and how it trickled over into my marriage (I was only a kid when I got married - really I was still in my 'dating age'). How confusing it was when guys wanted more than I was willing to give. It seemed like that was all they ever wanted. They never seemed to want to spend time with me for me, just sex or whatever they could get; which made me consider it because I really wanted them to like me, like other guys liked my friends. *Why did I date so little and why did some of my friends date a lot?* I felt inferior; I must be ugly or fat, why else would I be passed by? It wasn't until I was much older that I figured out that the reason my friends were so popular was that they did have sex. It may have never been that I was less desirable which was very important to me at the time – being desirable made me feel loved in a warped kind of way— it was that I wouldn't 'put out'. The saddest part about that twisted time in my life was that I believed that my value came from my friends and guys. They were the ones that got to decide my worth. I placed my tender heart and emotions in their hands." –J. (continued in Sex, Etc, Part Two)

Overflowing
1 John 1:5-10
1 Peter 5:6

Lord, I want to know Your truth. You have searched my heart. Teach me Your ways and then help me obey. Amen.

Sex, Etc. Part Two

If you're reading on after Part One, you have opened your heart to learn more about your Creator's perspective on sex. May He bless you and continually transform you through your teachable spirit. Here we go.

Just a few questions…

How would you define lust? (Webster defines it as, intense sexual desire; an intense longing; a craving.) _____
_____
_____
_____

Can you kiss a guy without thinking lustful thoughts about him? _____
_____
_____
_____

How long? How far does it go before you enter the lustful realm? _____
_____
_____

Thirsty?
Let's see what Jesus says to his disciples about the sin of lust in *Matthew 5:27-30:*

"You have heard that the law of Moses says, 'Do not commit adultery.' But I say, anyone who even looks at a woman with lust in his eye has already committed adultery with her in his heart. So if your eye—even if it is your good eye—causes you to lust, gouge it out and throw it away. It is better for you to lose one part of your body than for your whole body to be thrown into hell. And if your hand—even if it is your stronger hand—causes you to sin, cut it off and throw it away. It is better for you to lose one part of your body than for your whole body to be thrown into hell." (NLT)

Hold it. Don't mutilate yourself. I've paraphrased this in up-to-date language:

You have heard people at church say, "Don't have sex before marriage." But I say, anyone who sexually desires another person, has already been unfaithful to Me and to their (future) spouse. So, if things you watch or look at—even things you hold dear—cause you to think about sex, eliminate them. It is better for you to loose a temporary thing like a magazine, music, poster, book, movie or computer than to walk down the path that leads to destruction. And if the way you dress or talk or act causes you to sin, do everything you can to get rid of the action or lifestyle. It is better for you to lose something on this earth that will not last—even something/someone very dear to you, than to be separated from the most important thing: your relationship with Jesus that will last forever.

This is heavy stuff. You see, we serve an all or nothing God. Jesus cares so much about us, He doesn't want loopholes, excuses or a political agenda to rob us of the life He's called us to. He loves us enough to tell us the truth about life in this world. A person who hands you a condom, puts you on birth control, makes an empty promise or justifies acting on a sexual urge has settled for less than they were created for.

An intimate relationship outside of marriage can rob you of a full life in Jesus; not to mention all the other junk that goes with it: disease, shame, hurt, misunderstanding, no commitment, a hard heart.

So, where is the line? How far is too far? Look again at Matthew 5:27. Do we lust with thoughts, actions or both?

_____

_____

_____

When you are with a guy, how far can you go without lusting after him? _____

_____

_____

_____

What about him? Are your actions causing him to lust after you? What does the passage say about things that cause others to lust? _____

_____

_____

_____

_____

The Bible is very direct about sex because God knows it is powerful. It can bind people together. It can destroy people. The goal for us should be to stay as far away from the "lust line" as possible. If making out gets you close, then stay as far away from the line as possible—for your sake and the one you're with. If scenes in movies or music cause you to want to make out, back up another step. The more you eliminate to help your own mind and heart stay pure, the easier it will be to honor God on a daily basis.

Question to journal about:
Jesus, my King, what am I currently involved in that hurts You, me or someone else? Large or small, what can I eliminate to honor You and stay far from temptation? _____

_____
_____
_____
_____

Have you ever heard a married person say, "I really wish I had experimented more sexually before I got married?" It is a very difficult thing to tell the man you are *really* in love with that you gave a lot of yourself away in kisses, "I love you's" and physical acts that have scarred your heart. Remember, though, if Christ has given you a fresh start, then you are healing. He is making you new. Please do not beat yourself up over past mistakes. Confess it and enjoy receiving His forgiveness. (If you need to sort out some of your sin, go to the entries entitled, "Disgusting and Unaware" or "Sorrow or Guilt?") As you seek to live a pure life by removing obstacles from your path and not being an obstacle for someone else, you will experience great blessing that goes beyond words. See Acts 3:19-20.

Real Wisdom from Real Women
(continued from Sex, Etc. Part 1…)
    "The confusion over sex and my value lead to a lifetime of misunderstandings and a lifetime of 'missing it'. Oh, how I hate when I 'miss it'. I feel so cheated. I wish there would have been someone in my life who would have taken the time and been brave enough to set me straight. Of course, I did not ask either – I should have. First of all, my value has

never and does not come from another human. It comes from my God. And last time I checked He was pretty much in love with me. Secondly, in a marriage, sex is extremely important, it is a huge part of life; it should be wonderful for both the guy and the gal. It needs to be learned, practiced, and enjoyed. Sad to say I did not figure that out until I had been married for many years, 25 to be exact (talk about 'missing it')." –J.

Overflowing
Acts 3:19-20
1 Corinthians 6:13-20
Hebrews 12:25
Luke 17:1-5

Lord, let me know Your sweet embrace so that I can freely love others regardless of their pasts. Amen.

Sex, Etc. Part Three

I could tell you that I did not have sex before I was married, but does that mean I had a completely pure heart? My point here is that we all draw lines and try to rank ourselves by comparison to others. My dear sister, we are all under the cross. If you haven't been engaging in sex acts, I do commend you because you are growing up in a sex-crazed world. At the same time, I urge you to get on your knees and thank Jesus because it was He who gave you the strength. If you *have* done things you regret—large or small, I urge you to get on your knees and thank Jesus for saving you from it.

If there were a giant cross and all of the women who are reading this book collapsed before it in gratitude, there would be no line to stand on. I imagine we would all be hugging and so excited to know Jesus. As each new person came to join us and poured out her heart, would we say, "Honey, you've got nothing on me. What are *you* so broken about?" or "Oh, I never had that problem. I stayed away from that stuff." I believe that God's desire for us would be to hug her and point to Him. We are all under the cross together; all we can do is look up in gratitude and joy. Keep that picture in mind, because for the rest of your life you will encounter people with all different pasts. Do not let yourself be tempted to elevate or condemn yourself based on the choices of another person.

A few years ago, a group of high school kids I love dearly went on a youth retreat. We attended a session that had to do with sexual purity. The room was packed. The presenter shared all the horrible things that can come of sex before marriage. She knew more about diseases and the human body, than I care to know. Most kids in the room seemed to be pretty freaked out. That night over dinner, a guy from our group asked me if a person who had sex before marriage would go to hell. There was pain in his eyes. That led into a discussion among the people at our table. We talked about the truth and what Jesus came for.

Later that night during an evening session, I had to go up to the hotel room and he was sitting in the room alone. I asked him if he had asked the question for himself or for someone else. Huge tears filled his eyes and ran down his cheeks. From the eyes of the world, he was a good-looking, intelligent guy who was living it up in his high school years. In reality, he was dying inside.

In my heart I praised Jesus for convicting Him and pulling him off the road to hell and into His arms. I told him that what he did was wrong, but that is exactly why Jesus came. He came to free us from the prison of sin. He and I prayed together and God gave this guy a new heart and a huge hunger for His Word. Throughout the course of the year, he grew leaps and bounds. God used him to share the same message he received that night on a mission trip to Costa Rica the following summer.

My friend. Where are you? Are you sickened by choices you've made in the past or have you stayed sexually pure? It is possible that you have not acted on desires you have, but that you are not totally closed off to it either. **You may have not technically had sex, but you may have found outlets that are just as damaging to your soul and your relationship with Christ.**

What areas do you need to be covered by God's mercy?
_____
_____
_____
_____

Do you need to give God's mercy to others who are hurt by mistakes they've made? List a few people that you would like to pray for. _____
_____
_____
_____
_____

Will you surrender all of those memories of the past and let Christ pick you up and give you a fresh start? Will you let Him change your heart and your desires?

Raise your hands in surrender and talk to the One who loves you best...

O Lord, you are my rock of safety. Please help me; don't refuse to answer me. For if you are silent, I might as well give up and die. Listen to my prayer for mercy as I cry out to you for help, as I lift my hands toward your holy sanctuary. Psalm 28:1-2 (NLT)

What did He reveal to you as you prayed? _____
_____
_____
_____
_____
_____
_____

Thirsty?
When we are truly sorry for our sin and confess it, God cannot hold back from loving and forgiving us. Be encouraged by these verses:

If we say we have no sin, we are only fooling ourselves and refusing to accept the truth. But if we confess our sins to Him, He is faithful and just to forgive us and to cleanse us from every wrong. If we claim we have not sinned, we are calling God a liar and showing that this Word has no place in our hearts. I John 1:9 (NLT)

Come and listen, all you who fear God, and I will tell you what He did for me. For I cried out to Him for help, praising Him as I spoke. If I had not confessed the sin in my heart, my Lord would not have listened. But God did listen! He paid attention to my prayer. Praise God, who did not ignore my prayer and did not withdraw His unfailing love from me. Psalm 66:17-20 (NLT)

Praise the Lord! For He has heard my cry for mercy. The Lord is my strength, my shield from every danger. I trust in Him with all my heart. He helps me, and my heart is filled with joy. I burst out in songs of thanksgiving. Psalm 28:6-7 (NLT)

Real Wisdom from Real Women
(continued from Sex, Etc. Part Two)
"Here is the kicker: When I was young I was so caught up in seeking approval (value/worth) from my peers that I was connecting the urge (definitely was not a desire) to consider having sex to the longing to be loved and accepted. Makes sense to me now, but not then. Life is tough when you are a kid. And how should anyone be expected to just know these things? Truth is, there is no way to just know these things, unless you are told or you ask. One of the coolest things

about life is you get to meet people who have either been your age or you will eventually be their age. If we are wise we will always remember what it was like to be 'their' age and be willing to embrace the experiences of those whose age we will eventually be. You see it is inevitable, a sure thing. So why not live, learn and share as long as there are those who will listen, learn and live." –J.

Overflowing
2 Peter 2:4-14
2 Peter 3:11-18
Micah 6:8

God, help me to know and understand Your good intentions for me in regards to sex. Encourage me with Your blessings as I seek to obey You. Amen.

Sex, Etc. Part Four: More Good than Bad Reasons to Wait…

Here are some words from real people who did not have sex with their future spouse before they got married:

Hubby 1: "Every time you resist the temptation to have sex before you are married, you are investing into your married relationship. With each investment, the potential for an amazing return increases."

Wife 1: "I am so grateful to God that we were both committed to abstain while we dated. It seemed that when one of us was weak, the other was strong. I respect my husband so much for loving me enough to actually remind me of our commitment when I might have fallen. His self-control during our time of dating reassures me of his faithfulness to me now that we're married. We have an awesome love life—and we will soon be celebrating 10 years together. What a guy! I trust him, love him deeply and see how he models the love of Jesus to our family. I truly see that God asks us to wait because it is best for us. He's right. Fancy that!"

Hubby 2: "My wife and I decided when we were dating that we would not kiss before we got engaged. This was key for us because we had a long distance relationship and we wanted to make sure that when we were together, we were focusing on more than the physical part of our relationship. That commitment to purity really helped us set our relationship on a firm foundation. God honored that commitment and our obedience and has blessed us with an incredible marriage and partnership. We now have a lifetime to enjoy each other fully as a blessing from God."

Wife 2: "God said, 'and the two shall become one flesh.' He instituted it. He blesses it. IT is a beautiful thing, it is not meant to have shame and pain come with it. It is a special, wonderful gift. God in His goodness blesses it through grace. How awesome and blessed it is when we have been obedient. IT has layers and levels of goodness I can't put into words. Just trust Him, He is good. It brings new meaning to the old phrase 'good things come to those who wait'."

Thirsty?
Meditate on Psalm 1:

Oh, the joys of those who do not follow the advice of the wicked, or stand around with sinners, or join in with scoffers. But they delight in doing everything the LORD wants; day and night they think about His law. They are like trees planted along the riverbank, bearing fruit each season without fail. Their leaves never wither, and in all they do, they prosper. But this is not true of the wicked. They are like worthless chaff, scattered by the wind. They will be condemned at the time of judgment. Sinners will have no place among the godly. For the LORD watches over the path of the godly, but the path of the wicked leads to destruction. (NLT)

What promise does God give us about those who intentionally seek to obey Him? _____
_____
_____
_____

What is the picture of those who follow advice that rejects what scripture teaches? _____
_____
_____
_____

I'll admit there were plenty of times in my life when I've been on the right path and I felt like a big loser when I was around people who made other choices. It felt like I had a big ugly horn on my head. But…deep down inside somewhere, I felt God's quiet strength. I've later found that others didn't see a big ugly horn, but somewhere, deep down inside of them, they respected/envied me for my convictions. Things are not what they seem at times. With a lot of patience and endurance on your part, you will begin to see that you are bearing fruit and that God is blessing you for your obedience. Most likely, He's blessing you in ways you have never even thought of. Look for it.

How have you seen God making you like a tree that does not wither and prospers in everything? _____
_____
_____
_____
_____

What "horn on your head" experiences have you had that turned out to be a blessing in disguise? (For example, I can look back on a few times where I felt so left out of circles or parties when I was a teenager. I see now, that God was protecting me at a time when I might have been weak in obeying Him.)

_____
_____
_____
_____
_____
_____

Challenge: Begin to pray about your possible future spouse. You may even start to pray for him, asking the Lord to make him strong and to prepare your hearts for each other. If the Lord allows you to remain single, you may ask **Him** to be your soul mate and to let you find complete fulfillment in Him alone.

Real Wisdom from Real Women

"If you're not completely committed to not have sex before you're married, then you will." -Melissa

"It is better to be on the offense than the defense. Sex is a pure and sacred thing. Guard it. Save it. Ask yourself, 'How would my future husband feel if he saw me acting or talking this way with another guy?' Don't ask yourself, 'How far is too far?' How about, 'How much can I save *for* Him?' You will never regret it and he will be so blessed." -anonymous

Lord Jesus, give me Your perspective on repentance. Remove any unhealthy ideas I have about my sins. Amen.

Sorrow or Guilt?

I grew up hearing and saying, "I feel so guilty about... ." My whole family could tell you that we were masters at feeling guilty. We felt guilty about things we did, guilty about things we didn't do, guilty about not feeling guilty and so forth. Carrying guilt was just something we did second nature. During my college years, a wise professor asked me, "Does God want us to feel guilty about our sin?" My response was something like, "Probably, so that we won't commit the sin again." He gently corrected me by asking me the difference between sorrow and guilt. What *is* the difference, my friend? Let's take a look at scripture.

Thirsty?

For God can use sorrow in our lives to help us turn away from sin and seek salvation. We will never regret that kind of sorrow. But sorrow without repentance is the kind that results in death. 2 Corinthians 7:10

Yet now God in His gracious kindness declares us not guilty. He has done this through Christ Jesus, who has freed us by taking away our sins. Romans 3:24

That was a big "aha" moment. I had grown up letting Satan use guilt to imprison me. I knew somewhere in my mind that Christ had forgiven me, yet I believed somewhere in my heart that carrying guilt made me more repentant, or holy or something. Angela Thomas writes that guilt is a great weapon in the hands of Satan. He uses it to rob us of joy and move us into more 'doing' instead of 'being'. Ironically, I was carrying Satan's tool.

When we carry guilt, whose actions do we dishonor? (Reread Romans 3:24.) _____
_____
_____
_____

What does God use sorrow to produce in us? (Reread 2 Corinthians 7:10.) _____
_____
_____
_____

God wants us to confess our sin and then leave it behind. He already knows what we have done, but we need confession for *our* heart's sake. In confession, we acknowledge who we are and who Christ is. We give Him what we no longer want to carry. Confession softens our hearts. Guilt hardens and robs us of God's peace.

Take time to sit with pen in hand and ask God to produce healthy sorrow in you over sins you have not confessed. (You may use Colossians 3:5-11 to guide you.)
_____
_____
_____
_____
_____
_____

You see your sins on paper? Christ has saved you from those things. Let your spirit sing to Him for rescuing you. Write a prayer of thanksgiving and leave the guilt mantras behind. You are free to sing, walk, dance and "be" as He created you to be. Bask in this encouragement throughout your day.

___

Come and listen, all you who fear God, and I will tell you what He did for me. For I cried out to Him for help, praising Him as I spoke. If I had not confessed the sin in my heart, my Lord would not have listened. But God did listen! He paid attention to my prayer. Praise God, who did not ignore my prayer and did not withdraw His unfailing love for me. Psalm 66:16-20 (NLT)

Real Wisdom from Real Women
"Confessions of a Former Guilty Girl"

#1: "I feel guilty about some not-so-holy decisions I made when I was testing out my own path rather than the Way of the Lord some years ago. When I think about some of the things I did, I get this twang in my tummy, and believe me, it's not the butterfly kind. *Should I feel guilty?* NO!!! I already felt guilty years ago – because the Holy Spirit convicted me. I confessed my sins, asked for forgiveness and repented by turning away from those actions. If I continue to feel guilty, I am telling my Redeemer that I don't trust that He forgives me, cleanses me and forgets my sins. Our Savior's restoration of me wins over the condemnation of lingering guilt."

#2: "I feel guilty about not playing enough with my kids. *Should I feel guilty?* NO!!! I laid this guilt at Jesus' feet, and felt no conviction and no godly sorrow. I believe this is "false guilt" brought on by an unrealistic expectation I have of myself to be this picture-perfect mother. I probably got it from playing the comparison game with other moms (and Satan is the creator of THAT game). This worldly guilt doesn't make me play with my kids more – it simply paralyzes me. So I let Jesus free me from it, and amazingly, I think I am actually playing with my kids more! Our Savior's freeing me wins over the paralysis of false guilt."

#3: "I feel guilty for continually being so judgmental of my sister-in-law. *Should I feel guilty?* NO!!! But I do need to ask that our Fair Judge will turn that guilt into conviction through the Holy Spirit and give me godly sorrow for my sin. It is only when I feel true remorse that I can confess and repent. God is faithful and will forgive me and renew my mind and thoughts – and maybe lead me to hang out more with my sister-in-law. And so, our Savior's transformation of me wins over my strongholds. Don't drown yourself with guilt. Float in the restoring, releasing and transforming water of our Life Preserver." —Sue

Overflowing
Isaiah 43:25
Romans 3:21-31; 8:33-34
Psalm 32
Hebrews 9:13-14

Lord Jesus, help me to be honest with You in every area of my life and to truly desire to obey You. Teach me what Your desires are for me and help me to yield everything to You. Amen.

Temptation

I am not a psychologist. I am not sure of too many things in this difficult world. I will not quote statistics at you for your particular situation because I really don't know any. I can only humbly say that we *all* struggle with something. The Bible tells us that we will all be tempted; in fact we can count on it. It really doesn't matter how large or small the temptation may seem, if we are wrestling with any kind of evil, it is a dangerous and difficult thing. We can look at one another and size things up from the outside. We can believe, as the world does, that certain people have it all together and certain people don't. I've observed that those two categories are often decided upon based on appearance, especially weight or beauty. Unfortunately, it is easy for Christians living in this world to buy that and believe it of people they sit next to in church on Sunday morning. I have been guilty of thinking thoughts like that. The bottom line: Everyone is tempted. The struggle only gets easier when we recognize it and do all we can to avoid it.

What temptation do you struggle with on a regular basis?
_____
_____
_____

Have you noticed something you do that triggers the temptation? _____

_____
_____
_____

In what ways has God provided a way out for you? If you have not recognized it yet, from this point forward look for it and thank Him when you see Him at work.

_____
_____
_____

I am certain though, that whatever you struggle with, there is a way out in Jesus Christ. I am convinced that whatever your issue, God wants to use it to draw you to Himself and **He will** as you let Him. Many well-meaning people may tell you that your issue is okay or that we are sinful people and you will not have the strength to overcome. False. Do not settle for a mediocre life. We may stumble, but with Jesus, all things are possible! Let's devour this scripture:

So, if you think you are standing firm, be careful that you don't fall! No temptation has seized you except what is common to man. And God is faithful; He will not let you be tempted beyond what you can bear. But when you are tempted, He will also provide a way out so that you can stand up under it. 1 Corinthians 10:12-13

There are three basic principles in this scripture that we can learn from a Father who knows His children better than we know ourselves.

1. Don't think for a minute that you have mastered a temptation or can go on in life without being in step

with Jesus and praying to Him constantly. Scripture says it is that kind of thinking that will send us falling on our faces!
2. You will never have some sort of unique temptation that no one else has ever dealt with.
3. God will never let you down. When you are tempted, He will always provide a way out. Look for it and don't give in to your own desires.

If you are struggling with seemingly huge temptations, let God draw you in. He wants to walk with you—remember *Jesus is the only one to walk this earth and overcome every temptation possible.* Hear me, please. If you battle an eating disorder, sexual sins: lesbian or heterosexual, an abusive relationship, hatred, self-condemnation, an addiction—sexual or drug/alcohol, pride or gossip, you are not alone and you are not without the help and victory of the Most High God. If I were sitting in a coffee shop with you discussing whatever temptation you battle, I would pray this prayer with you. Pray it now and ask God to help you stand.

Lord Jesus, give me strength to daily overcome_____. I recognize that there is no way I can do this on my own. God, help me to clearly see and know when I am being tempted to yield to evil. Help me to see the way out that You have provided me. Send someone in my life to pray with me and to help keep me accountable. When You give me victory, help me to remember to praise You and not let go of Your hand. I trust You. Amen.

Thirsty?

This High Priest [Jesus] of ours understands our weaknesses, for He faced all of the same temptations we do, yet He did not sin. So let us come boldly to the throne of our gracious

God. There we will receive His mercy, and we will find grace to help us when we need it. Hebrews 4:15-16 (NLT)

So humble yourselves before God. Resist the Devil, and he will flee from you. Draw close to God, and God will draw close to you. Wash your hands, you sinners; purify your hearts, you hypocrites. Let there be tears for the wrong things you have done. Let there be sorrow and deep grief. Let there be sadness instead of laughter, and gloom instead of joy. When you bow down before the Lord and admit your dependence on Him, He will lift you up and give you honor. James 4:7-10 (NLT)

So take a new grip with your tired hands and stand firm on your shaky legs. Mark out a straight path for your feet. Then those who follow you, though they are weak and lame, will not stumble and fall but will become strong. Hebrews 12: 12-13 (NLT)

Challenge: When you recognize that you're being tempted, look for the way out that God has provided for you. Talk to Him about it and then experience His victory by taking His way out. This may be a minute-to-minute process at first, but you will gain strength in Jesus and self-discipline that will only help you in the future.

Real Wisdom from Real Women
"I know that in this age, sexual sin is extremely difficult to overcome. We are bombarded with images and subtle or blatant messages almost everywhere we turn. Yet, God promises a way out. The world has never had such a selection of Christian music, books, movies and resources as this generation does. Perhaps in this time of testing, that is God's way out. He is providing us a new path. We are given a choice: To walk through the evil and entertain its ways or

take the unique road that He has carved for us. That is what it comes down to: shutting off the television, switching the station, blocking a site, reading a book that pours life into our souls." –A.

Overflowing
Philippians 4:8
Hebrews 12:1-4
James 1:12-17
Psalm 34
Psalm 37:23-24

Lord Jesus, speak to me through Your Word. I yield to Your direction. Open my eyes and give me the strength to obey You. Amen.

Renewed Commitments, Renewed Strength

Take time to read this passage in scripture. With pen in hand, mark the phrases that jump out at you. Resist the temptation to glance over it. These are words of life...

Therefore, since we are surrounded by such a huge crowd of witnesses to the life of faith, let us strip off every weight that slows us down, especially the sin that so easily hinders our progress. And let us run with endurance the race that God has set before us. We do this by keeping our eyes on Jesus, on whom our faith depends from start to finish. He was willing to die a shameful death on the cross because of the joy He knew would be His afterward. Now He is seated in the place of highest honor beside God's throne in heaven. Think about all He endured when sinful people did such terrible things to Him, so that you don't become weary and give up. After all, you have not yet given your lives in your struggle against sin.

And have you entirely forgotten the encouraging words God spoke to you, His children? He said, "My child, don't ignore it when the Lord disciplines you, and don't be discouraged when He corrects you. For the Lord disciplines those He loves, and He punishes those He accepts as His children."

As you endure this divine discipline, remember that God is treating you as His own children. Whoever heard of a child who was never disciplined? If God doesn't discipline you as He does all of his children, it means that you are illegitimate and are not really His children after all. Since we respect our earthly fathers who disciplined us, should we not all the more cheerfully submit to the discipline of our heavenly Father and live forever?

For our earthly fathers disciplined us for a few years, doing the best they knew how. But God's discipline is always right and good for us because it means we will share in His holiness. No discipline is enjoyable while it is happening—it is painful! But afterward there will be a quiet harvest of right living for those who are trained in this way.

So take a new grip with your tired hands and stand firm on your shaky legs. Mark out a straight path for your feet. Then those who follow you, though they are weak and lame, will not stumble and fall but will become strong. Hebrews 10:1-13 (NLT)

Has our gracious God been counseling you? Are you moved to make some changes or to add a few things to your commitment list? Are you on the "I have a boyfriend and it's moving too fast train"? For the glory of God and for the way you were created—derail that trail, sister! I remember after a mission trip, I was so immersed in God and excited to go home and share hundreds of things that God had done. We were at a debriefing session and Ron Luce, the speaker, was urging us to end relationships that were not beneficial to our spiritual life. It was just the nudge I needed. I committed to end a long distance relationship. My parents and close friends were surprised because he was a really good guy. There was nothing that seemed bad about me occasionally dating him. I knew deep down in my heart that God did not want me to be tied to anyone and that all I really needed was to focus on Him. You see, your job at this time in your life is to use your freedom to honor God and develop and use the gifts He's given you. Think about it: You most likely are not paying a rent or mortgage on a house, you have your summers and school breaks free—this is the time to really take opportunities and fly.

It is crucial that your walk with God become a real and exciting walk. It's up to you to make it real; He's the one who makes it exciting. There are a few things that need to happen, as you read each one, make notes about how you will personally implement these changes:

Be aware of your weak areas. *What are they?*
_____
_____
_____

Eliminate anything that will make you want to be weak. *What will I get rid of?* _____
_____
_____
_____

Carve productive time out of each day for you and God to get to know each other. *What is my best time of day?*
_____
_____

Be open and honest about all the little ways that you fail and be quick to embrace His forgiveness and keep moving.

Only look back on your past to be gracious to others who have fallen, not to beat yourself up. How can I use my testimony

to bless others? Will I be honest about past mistakes so that God can have the glory? _____
_____
_____
_____

If you haven't already, find a mentor. (See "A Seasoned Sister") *Who is a mature Christian that I can trust?*
_____
_____
_____

Enjoy being alone. Use much of your alone time to develop your own unique gifts. *How has God created me uniquely?* (See "Younique") _____
_____
_____
_____
_____
_____

Meditate on and memorize scripture often. Start with Philippians 2:13 (My paraphrase).

For it is God who is at work within me, giving me the will and power to achieve His purpose.

The only part we can do is renew our commitments, and trust God to provide the strength. We can draw strength from Him, but we cannot resist evil on our own. Actually, that's when we fall. Put yourself in a position to allow God to speak life in your soul. Here are some ideas:

- **Regular church attendance**
- Time:
- Youth group meeting time:

- **Christian music**
- Radio stations in your area:
- Artists that produce your style:

- **Group Bible study**
- When:

- **Keep a journal to God**
- Get one today!

I am praying for you. May you sing this verse in your heart all day:

But I trust in your unfailing love; my heart rejoices in your salvation. I will sing to the Lord, for He has been good to me. Psalm 13:5-6 (NLT)

Real Wisdom from Real Women

"In order for you to understand your temptations, weaknesses and needs, you have to take the time to understand yourself. With two beautiful older sisters, I was constantly trying to prove that I was grown up. One of the ways that I pursued this was to enter into a serious relationship when I was only 15. This relationship lasted through the majority of my high school years.

"Looking back, I realize that I was putting the concerns, needs and interests of my boyfriend over my own.....and God's. I know now that I do not like to watch hockey, but I didn't seem to know it then. I am not a big fan of the color purple (well the movie yes, the color no). He was. I wore purple dresses to 2 high school dances. These are not life and death situations, just silly examples of how easy it is to change for someone..... without even knowing it's happening. Although I am still friends with my high school beau, I realize now how much time and effort I put into someone else's hobbies and interests. I do not mean to imply that young women cannot have true feelings for a boyfriend. In fact, part of me was attempting to prove to people who said 'High School relationships don't mean anything' or 'It's just puppy love' that I could and did have those feelings. Instead, I want to tell you that there is a good chance that you will be married someday and will share the interests, hobbies and needs of your husband and children for the rest of your life. I am married to a wonderful man and I am doing just that now. But our marriage has been more difficult because my spiritual growth was stunted. Pleasing someone else left little or no room for inner reflection. Where should I set boundaries? Do I think that behavior was disrespectful? Is this a battle I should pick? What is my favorite color? How can I give my all to my husband, when I am not even sure what that is? Learning and growing spiritually will be slowed down dramatically if you are living for someone other than Christ —this can be friends as well as boyfriends. Your life won't get any less hectic. Backtracking to find God's purpose for you is as practical as watching hockey in a purple prom dress." –Kirsten (my amazing little sister)

Overflowing
Ephesians 5:15-20; 6:10-18
Psalm 119:37

Good morning, Jesus. I seek You alone today. Wake me with Your Spirit and refresh me with Your Word. Amen.

Idols

Thirsty?

¹⁴But the Israelites would not listen. They were as stubborn as their ancestors and refused to believe in the LORD their God. ¹⁵They rejected his laws and the covenant he had made with their ancestors, and they despised all his warnings. They worshiped worthless idols and became worthless themselves. They followed the example of the nations around them, disobeying the LORD's command not to imitate them. ¹⁶They defied all the commands of the LORD their God and made two calves from metal. They set up an Asherah pole and worshiped Baal and all the forces of heaven. ¹⁷They even sacrificed their own sons and daughters in the fire. They consulted fortune-tellers and used sorcery and sold themselves to evil, arousing the LORD's anger. 2 Kings 17:14-17 (NLT)

The Bible has so many examples of idol worship. Have you ever wondered what it must have been like? More than once I have wanted to travel back to the ancient world to try to grasp what was so fabulous about a lifeless figure. In simple terms, a person or entire group of people would form an idol out of stone, metal or wood, make up a name for it and then worship it by following a list of rules that they made up. It seems a little crazy, doesn't it? They would actually let their lives revolve around something made-up. How could they be motivated to do so? Didn't they realize that a person made it? What would it take for any person to devote his or her whole life, attitude and heart to a block of wood, stone or metal?

[Did you know that when the Bible mentions Asherah poles, it refers to the Babylonian goddess of fertility. In order to honor "her" they would actually have sex in group orgies before it. Baal was another idol that was worshipped in the Old Testament. Many people would offer their babies as a sacrifice.]

The reason God had such a problem with idol worship is that it alienated His people from Him.

1 Corinthians 10 says that when people worshiped idols, they were actually worshipping demons. That is a serious offense with deadly consequences. The bottom line is that idolatry is giving time, attention, money and credence to something other than God. When you really think about it, have things changed all that much? Perhaps if we traveled back in time, things would not look much different from today.

What things (time, attention, money, etc.) do we put before God? _____
_____
_____
_____
_____
_____

Do you feel yourself being pressured to worship any "idols" today? What made-up rules do you find yourself trying to obey?_____
_____
_____
_____
_____

There are probably billions of different idols that we have bowed before in this world. Some examples may be: hatred, extra sleep, a boyfriend, tolerance, intolerance, unhealthy friendships, TV, movies, pornography, your image, approval of others, money, job, vanity, bitterness, a political agenda, selfish-ambition, lack of motivation, an eating disorder, pride... . It really doesn't matter the size of the idol, what matters is that it stands between you and your life-giving Heavenly Father. Perhaps you have two or three that you listen to, perhaps there are more. Be sure though, that there is one enemy. Satan is the enemy of your Lord and Savior Jesus Christ and he will use anything in his power to rob you of the amazing, purpose-filled life that Jesus has for you.

What was the result of the idol worship in the Bible? (Take another look at 2 Kings 17:15.)_____
_____
_____
_____

It seems pretty logical, doesn't it? If we follow something that's pointless, our lives will reflect that pointlessness. Do you know what God's people did when they realized their sin? They confessed their sin, smashed their idols and ran back to their Heavenly Father.

It is impossible for God to work mightily in us when we are bowing before a worthless something. *2 Corinthians 6:16* says, *"What agreement is there between the temple of God and idols? For we are the temple of the living God. As God has said: I will live among them and walk among them, and I will be their God, and they will be my people."*

What idols do you need to smash? List each one and how you plan to eliminate it from your life. If you need help eliminating something that you struggle with, seek out a Christian counselor, mentor or an adult who is serious about their walk with Jesus (See "A Seasoned Sister"). If your idols are not obvious to you, ask God to reveal what keeps you from knowing Him. He loves you enough to let you know what stands in the way of His care. _____

_____
_____
_____
_____

The best part is, your Heavenly Father holds His arms wide open for you. The Bible says that He is *jealous* for us. He adores you enough to make a way for you to come to Him through the sacrifice of Jesus. No idol can speak gently to you, defend you, forgive you or love you like that.

Let the apostle Paul's words sink into your heart:

So, my dear friends, flee from the worship of idols. You are reasonable people. Decide for yourselves if what I am about to say is true. When we bless the cup at the Lord's Table, aren't we sharing in the benefits of the blood of Christ? And when we break the loaf of bread, aren't we sharing in the benefits of the body of Christ? And we all eat from one loaf, showing that we are one body. And think about the nation of Israel; all who eat the sacrifices are united by that act.

What am I trying to say? Am I saying that the idols to whom the pagans bring sacrifices are real gods and that these sacrifices are of some value? No, not at all. What I am saying is that these sacrifices are offered to demons, not to God. And I don't want any of you to be partners with demons. You cannot drink from the cup of the Lord and from the cup of demons, too. You cannot eat at the Lord's Table and at the table of demons, too. What? Do you dare to rouse the Lord's jealousy as Israel did? Do you think we are stronger than He is? 1 Corinthians 10:14-22 (NLT)

Please pray with me...

Lord, thank You for making us aware of idols in our lives. Thank You for rescuing us from worthlessness. Open our eyes to things that will separate us from You and give us the strength and desire to flee from them. Fill us with Your purpose, Your life and Your peace. Amen.

Real Wisdom from Real Women
"Let us remember that we're in a battle for souls. The father of lies wants nothing more than to keep our eyes and thoughts off the Kingdom of God and get us to focus on things of this world." — Jessi

Overflowing
1 Corinthians 10 (read all of it)
Psalm 40:4-17
Psalm 115:2-8
Isaiah 40:18-31

Lord Jesus, create in me the qualities that will make me even more beautiful in Your eyes, and help me to desire them above all. Amen.

Picture of a Woman of God

Do you ever find yourself wondering what kind of woman you are supposed to be? Do you find yourself trying to figure out which character you are most like in a movie or book? Do you try to figure out how others view you? I can relate. I felt pretty set free as I began to realize that I don't have to be anything close to a fictional character nor do I have to fit into a category at all, nor do I have to be a little of everything. Tomboy, jock, plastic, glamour, angel, demon-girl or smarty—we can just "be" and let God our Creator bring out what He wants in us as we come to know Him. As He brings out His creation in us, He will enable us to embrace ourselves as women in His kingdom. It is possible to humbly love ourselves because we realize that it isn't about us at all. It's about *us* being part of *His* gorgeous creation and divine plan.

Let's take a good look at a truly beautiful woman of God. In this chapter, Luke gives us examples of two women who loved the Lord and sought to honor Him in the lives He gave them. If you know the story, do not be tempted to skim it. Ask God to draw you in to portions that He wants you to learn and let Him counsel you as you study.

Thirsty?

²⁶*In the sixth month, God sent the angel Gabriel to Nazareth, a town in Galilee,* ²⁷*to a virgin pledged to be married to a man named Joseph, a descendant of David. The virgin's name was Mary.* ²⁸*The angel went to her and said, "Greetings, you who are highly favored! The Lord is with you."*
²⁹*Mary was greatly troubled at his words and wondered what kind of greeting this might be.* ³⁰*But the angel said to her, "Do not be afraid, Mary, you have found favor with God.* ³¹*You will be with child and give birth to a son, and you are to give him the name Jesus.* ³²*He will be great and will be called the Son of the Most High. The Lord God will give him the throne of his father David,* ³³*and he will reign over the house of Jacob forever; his kingdom will never end."*
³⁴*"How will this be," Mary asked the angel, "since I am a virgin?"* ³⁵*The angel answered, "The Holy Spirit will come upon you, and the power of the Most High will overshadow you. So the holy one to be born will be called the Son of God.* ³⁶*Even Elizabeth your relative is going to have a child in her old age, and she who was said to be barren is in her sixth month.* ³⁷*For nothing is impossible with God."*
³⁸ *"I am the Lord's servant," Mary answered. "May it be to me as you have said." Then the angel left her.*
³⁹*At that time Mary got ready and hurried to a town in the hill country of Judea,* ⁴⁰*where she entered Zechariah's home and greeted Elizabeth.* ⁴¹*When Elizabeth heard Mary's greeting, the baby leaped in her womb, and Elizabeth was filled with the Holy Spirit.* ⁴²*In a loud voice she exclaimed: "Blessed are you among women, and blessed is the child you will bear!* ⁴³*But why am I so favored, that the mother of my Lord should come to me?* ⁴⁴*As soon as the sound of your greeting reached my ears, the baby in my womb leaped for joy.* ⁴⁵*Blessed is she who has believed that what the Lord has said to her will be accomplished!"* ⁴⁶*And Mary said: "My soul glorifies the*

Lord [47] and my spirit rejoices in God my Savior, [48] for He has been mindful of the humble state of His servant. From now on all generations will call me blessed, [49] for the Mighty One has done great things for me— holy is His name. [50] His mercy extends to those who fear Him, from generation to generation. [51] He has performed mighty deeds with His arm; He has scattered those who are proud in their inmost thoughts. [52] He has brought down rulers from their thrones but has lifted up the humble. [53] He has filled the hungry with good things but has sent the rich away empty. [54] He has helped His servant Israel, remembering to be merciful [55] to Abraham and His descendants forever, even as He said to our fathers." [56] Mary stayed with Elizabeth for about three months and then returned home. Luke 1:26-56 (NLT)

Interesting. The text says nothing of Mary's appearance, yet we, along with every artist throughout history assume she must have been beautiful. It is possible that she could have had a weight problem, acne or some sort of deformity and found favor with the Most High God. She may have been a looker. Yet, God in His Sovereign wisdom tells us nothing of how she was viewed on the outside. We know from 1 Samuel 16:7 that, *"The Lord does not look at the things man looks at. Man looks at the outward appearance, but the Lord looks at the heart."* So what heart qualities are revealed in Luke about this inwardly beautiful woman? See if you can discover them in the verse numbers listed:

v. 1:27 _____

v. 1:28 _____

v. 1:30 _____

v. 1:32 _____

v. 1:38 _____

v. 1:45 _____

v. 1:46-56 _____

What did you find as you studied? I was amazed to see a young girl surrounded by God's presence. We know that she was obedient because she was a virgin—even when she was engaged. She found favor with God in her daily actions. Due to a close walk with God, she trusted Him with a huge task: to bear the Son of the Most High God, whose kingdom will never end! (v.32) She also yielded to His command and His call, by humbly answering, "I am the Lord's servant." Mary believed that God was going to do what He said He was gong to do and then freely worshipped Him.

These qualities do not have to be unique to Mary. In fact, **intimacy, obedience, faith, submission and an active worship life** are what God desires of all of us. They are gifts that He offers. Will we, as women who know Him, embrace what He's doing in us and accept the task of honoring Him in all we do?

He isn't looking for someone with a flawless face or figure, a hero or shining star. He is not looking for someone who competes with a man or stands out in a crowd. He looks for lowly servant girls who love Him. If you possess beautiful outer qualities and abilities, great, but I encourage you to go for much more. May you embrace who you are, regardless of how others view you because God, your Creator, embraced you first.

Take some time to ask God to develop in you the qualities you read about today. Specifically list the ones that you have been lacking. Watch how He works miraculous answers to your heartfelt prayers.

The qualities I prayed for: _____
_____
_____
_____
_____

Real Wisdom from Real Women
"God made Adam. God made Eve. God made man. God made woman. He needed both—not just Adam and not just Eve, but *together* they were created. Eve completed the picture. If man alone were sufficient for the world, God would not have created Eve. She had a specific role, a specific purpose. And so do you.

The pieces of a woman are like pieces of a puzzle. God gives us our intelligence, our nurturing souls, our beauty, our organization, our humor, our industriousness, our faith, our joy, our love…all to be pieced together to form a woman. It is our responsibility to develop each of our pieces to their fullest. But God's will for us is not solely to develop ourselves. Nor does He want us to develop ourselves according to what the world values and esteems. Rather, He wants us to develop ourselves to serve Him as only a woman can. Piece together the pieces you have been given to be a daughter of your Lord.

Being loving and affectionate is ok. You can still be strong.

Being humble and serving others will make you more of a leader than you can imagine.

Being a devoted and tender wife makes you feel whole.

Being a mom is the greatest joy you will ever know.

Living as His beloved daughter will bring you more peace than you think possible.

Listening to your King will bring you the freedom to embrace being a woman." —Sue

Overflowing
Luke 1:5-80
Galatians 5

Lord Jesus, Remind me that I am in Your grip. Let me feel Your presence and Your arms around me today. Amen.

The Perfect Dad

If you could imagine the best father in the world, what would he be like? List some characteristics he would have.

_____
_____
_____
_____

How would you relate to him?
- ❏ Wait for him to seek you out
- ❏ Crawl on his lap and let him hold you
- ❏ Let him pass on knowledge and skills to you
- ❏ Sit on his shoulders to see the world from his perspective
- ❏ Plead with him when you need or want something
- ❏ Ask him for advice
- ❏ Let him fight your battles with/for you
- ❏ Confide in him
- ❏ Be open about your weaknesses
- ❏ Celebrate your successes
- ❏ Trust that he provides what you need

You may have a wonderful father who models the characteristics you listed above or you may have a difficult time even picturing what it would be like to have a tender, committed father. The Bible often compares God's love to that of a compassionate Father. Many people have kept God at a distance because they have been so hurt by their own earthly father and cannot fathom a God who loves them unconditionally. Yet, God's very nature makes Him vastly different from what we experience in this world. This is what the Bible says about His feelings for you:

Thirsty?

"See how very much our heavenly Father loves us, for He allows us to be called His children, and we really are! But the people who belong to this world don't know God, so they don't understand that we are His children. Yes, dear friends, we really are God's children, and we can't even imagine what we will be like when Christ returns. But we do know that when He comes we will be like Him, for we will see Him as He really is." I John 3:1-2 (NLT)

"As a mother comforts her child, so will I comfort you..." Isaiah 66:13

"Then you will call, and the Lord will answer; you will cry for help and He will say: Here am I." Isaiah 58:9

*"Can a mother forget the baby at her breast and have no compassion on the child she has borne? Though she may forget, **I will not** forget you! See, I have engraved you on the palms of my hands..." Isaiah 49:15-16 (accent added)*

"Fear not, for I have redeemed you; I have summoned you by name; you are mine." Isaiah 43:1

The Lord your God is with you, He is mighty to save. He will take great delight in you, He will quiet you with His love, He will rejoice over you with singing. Zephaniah 3:17

The LORD your God is going ahead of you. He will fight for you, just as you saw him do in Egypt. And you saw how the LORD your God cared for you all along the way as you traveled through the wilderness, just as a father cares for his child. Now he has brought you to this place. Deuteronomy 1:30-31 (NLT)

So you should not be like cowering, fearful slaves. You should behave instead like God's very own children, adopted into His family—calling Him "Father, dear Father." For His Holy Sprit speaks to us deep in our hearts and tells us that we are God's children. And since we are His children, we will share His treasures—for everything God gives to His Son, Christ, is ours, too. But if we are to share His glory, we must also share His suffering. Yet what we suffer now is nothing compared to the glory He will give us later. Romans 8:15-18 (NLT)

I have tears in my eyes as I type these verses because you may not know how precious you are to God. So many women go through life with so much pain, unaware that their Heavenly Father wants to cradle them in His arms. Are you that young woman? Have you let Him hold you? Let Him wipe the tears from your eyes and heal your heart. He says to you, "You are Mine."

If you have been abused, neglected or abandoned by your earthly father, ask your heavenly Father to show you what a pure relationship with Him is like. Ask Him to put Christian mentors in your life to help you heal. It may take time, but your heavenly Father is patient and kind and He is faithful. Healing is a process. Cherish the time He specially leads you and teaches you as you work through painful memories or difficult times.

Take as much time as you need to talk to your heavenly Daddy. Let Him tell you how much He adores you. You can never bother Him or take up too much time. He values you enough to give His very own Son for you. Tell Him your sins, your hopes your dreams, your disappointments.

Take a minute to write about your time in prayer with Him. What have you experienced? _____
_____
_____
_____
_____
_____
_____
_____

Challenge: Choose a passage from above and write it on an index card or small piece of paper with your name inserted. Memorize it throughout the day and remember that you are adored.

Real Wisdom from Real Women

"It always strikes me when someone says, "God doesn't care about little things; He has bigger things to worry about." When someone makes that statement, I get the impression that they don't picture God as a Father, but rather a distant being, unconcerned and too busy to care about His children. I often say that God most definitely cares about the little things, but that we choose not to see these little miracles. How disappointed that must make God feel.

Years ago when I was in college, I had gotten off work and was quite hungry. I was a poor college student and only had enough change in my car to purchase a hamburger and a water at a local Burger King. While I was sitting in the drive-thru line, I thought to myself, 'Boy, I would love it if I could have a chocolate milkshake;' however, I knew I couldn't afford one. When I arrived at the window to pick up my hamburger, the attendant told me that a customer had just driven through and didn't want his large chocolate milkshake and the attendant asked me if I wanted it (for free). I immediately got tears in my eyes and rambled to the attendant that I had just wanted one, but didn't have enough money, exclaiming that God provided me with this amazing blessing. Who knows what she thought of me! Just think: without me asking or without me having any resentment about not having the money, God as my Father blessed me out of the blue. He cares about every aspect in our lives, from the surprise parking space that appears, to even milkshakes.

Even though it has been many years since this happened, I have always remembered God touching me in this little way and how personal that was for me. Now, as I get older and life is moving more quickly, I have to make myself slow down to witness these little blessings from our Father, so specific to me as His child. I encourage you to look for these "little" miracles in your life and thank God for knowing you so intimately that even your smallest concern is His concern. Remember: It's not your burden to decide if God is too busy for you. It is your *blessing* to open your eyes and witness the miracles from big to small, which He pours onto you each day. All we have to do as a loving child, is to reach up our arms to our Dad, holding onto His neck, looking into His eyes and accepting the blessings. He is not a far away being, but a loving Father who cares about parking spaces, milkshakes, protecting you from an accident, what line we go into at the grocery store, etc. I'm sure that your list will certainly surpass mine.

Thank you Lord, for being my loving Father, loving me unconditionally and only wanting the best for every aspect of my life. Thank you for all of the miracles you have given and all the more you are planning to bestow. Daddy, please open my eyes to see you as my loving Father. I know that you have all the time for me in the world. I praise you for all that I am about to see- with no earthly limits or conditions. Abba Father Amen."

      Love, Your little girl, Heidi
      (My wonderful big sister)

Overflowing
Romans 8
Psalm 91
John 10:11-18

There are so many verses about God's love. List some of your favorites here.

_____
_____
_____
_____
_____
_____
_____
_____

Lord Jesus, I want to love You above all. Quiet my heart as I sit at Your feet today. Amen.

One Thing

Circle some of the things that consume most of your time:

Sports   Job   Friendships   Boyfriend

Homework   Church activities   Going out

Time with Jesus   School   Other

Of the ones you chose, which are you most personally committed to? _____
_____
_____
_____

    During my sophomore year of college, I represented my home county, by making appearances, speaking to groups and assisting with presentations at our local fair. I prayed that God would give me a chance to witness Him to others because I really believed He had blessed me with this opportunity. One night, a friend of my fathers' who was a strong Christian, was hosting a public event. He told my dad to let me know that he would ask me about my mission trips so that I could share my heart for Jesus with those in the crowd.

I made sure I looked very nice and looked forward to sharing a bit about my trips. However, I had been so busy "doing" that I really slacked in my time with God. That evening, there were probably two hundred people in the crowd and he asked me, "Anneke, I understand you've gone on several mission trips..." I replied, "Yes, I spent a month in Nicaragua and a month in Ukraine." "What is something you've learned from these experiences?" he asked. Here was my big chance, yet I responded with some empty answer like, "You can really learn a lot from traveling. It's a great experience." I blew it. When I got home, I sobbed because it was through my mission trips that I became passionate for Jesus. He taught me self-sacrifice, compassion, the importance of Bible study and prayer on a daily basis, passionate worship and on and on. Somewhere deep in my heart I had fantastic things to share about Jesus. To this day, I am disappointed in my answer, but our merciful God gently showed me what went wrong: I missed out on time with Him. For most of that week I had missed my quiet times. I was not spilling over with His love, because I had not been with Him. I got so caught up in serving Jesus that I missed *Him*.

Think of a time when you missed the big picture. What did you sacrifice? _____
_____
_____

Thirsty?

As Jesus and the disciples continued on their way to Jerusalem, they came to a village where a woman named Martha welcomed them into her home. Her sister, Mary, sat at the Lord's feet, listening to what He taught. But Martha was worrying about the big dinner she was preparing. She came to Jesus and said, "Lord, doesn't it seem unfair to you that my sister just sits here while I do all the work? Tell her to come and help me." But the Lord said to her, "My dear Martha, you are upset over all these details! There is really one thing worth being concerned about. Mary has discovered it and I won't take it away from her." Luke 10:38-41 (NLT)

Who was Jesus teaching when He arrived at Martha's home? _____
_____
_____

From what you know about the culture in the Middle East, what sort of response is expected from Jesus as He teaches the disciples? What would most male teachers say to a woman who joined a group of men? _____
_____
_____

What does this account tell us about Jesus' heart for Mary and Martha? _____
_____
_____
_____

What does this tell you about Jesus' passion and concern for you personally? _____
_____
_____
_____

How do we, even with good intentions, miss Jesus?

What is the result of missing Jesus? We may turn into a self-righteous Martha, we may become frustrated because deep down we know that there must be something more to being a Christian, or we may just become empty, ineffective servants until we repent and realize that we did not start our endeavor with the most needed thing: forgiveness, love and wisdom at the feet of Jesus.

We can have the best intentions in the world. We may be serving Christ with all that we are, but if He is not with us on our adventure, teaching us, guiding us, molding us and pouring into us, our work is pointless. We must never let the things in this world distort our spiritual view. The only way we are saved from spiritual distortion is by allowing Christ to pour into us and nudge us to act.

I used to feel sorry for Martha when I read this story. It seemed to me like Jesus did not appreciate her or that He liked Mary better. I have since changed my mind. I believe that His words were not harsh. He probably loved the meal that she prepared for Him, but what I believe He longed for much more than a delicious meal and a perfect-looking home, was Martha herself. I imagine when the all-knowing God peered into her eyes, He was communicating, "Martha, you are worth so much more to me than service."

When we serve our Lord purely out of devotion and adoration for what He is constantly teaching us, we serve with joy. We do not have to be bitter or frustrated about the level of service of others. We serve an audience of One. And *that*, my friends is the treasure.

Take some time to journal your thoughts to Him…

Real Wisdom from Real Women

"Help me Lord, to spend my days the way I should: striving to be the person You want me to be, not the person I want to be or the person *I think* I should be. Amen." –Joy

"Sit down. Let's just visit. We can always wash dishes. Have you ever noticed they don't run away?"—Esther *(These are words from my sweet grandma when I would come to visit. I always feel I am a priority because she makes time to be with me.)*

Lord God, give me the wisdom to know when to speak so that You may be glorified. Then, give me the strength to stand. Amen.

Still Standing

I am so excited to share this story. It may seem like an old Sunday School tale, but do not be duped. This story really happened. It is about three young people who loved God so passionately, they were willing to be humiliated in front of mobs and they were God-gutsy before a powerful King. Read it and enjoy it. I encourage you to highlight the portions you are most amused or moved by. Imagine you are thousands of years back in time and miles away in the godless country of Babylon…

Thirsty?

King Nebuchadnezzar made a gold statue ninety feet tall and nine feet wide and set it up on the plain of Dura in the province of Babylon. Then he sent messages to the princes, prefects, governors, advisers, counselors, judges, magistrates, and all the provincial officials to come to the dedication of the statue he had set up. When all these officials had arrived and were standing before the image King Nebuchadnezzar had set up, a herald shouted out, "People of all races and nations and languages, listen to the king's command! When you hear the sound of the horn, flute, zither, lyre, harp, pipes, and other instruments, bow to the ground to worship King

Nebuchadnezzar's gold statue. Anyone who refuses to obey will immediately be thrown into a blazing furnace."

So at the sound of the musical instruments, all the people, whatever their race or nation or language, bowed to the ground and worshiped the statue that King Nebuchadnezzar had set up.

But some of the astrologers went to the king and informed on the Jews. They said to King Nebuchadnezzar, "Long live the king! You issued a decree requiring all the people to bow down and worship the gold statue when they hear the sound of the musical instruments. That decree also states that those who refuse to obey must be thrown into a blazing furnace. But there are some Jews—Shadrach, Meshach, and Abednego—whom you have put in charge of the province of Babylon. They have defied Your Majesty by refusing to serve your gods or to worship the gold statue you have set up."

Then Nebuchadnezzar flew into a rage and ordered Shadrach, Meshach, and Abednego to be brought before him. When they were brought in, Nebuchadnezzar said to them, "Is it true, Shadrach, Meshach, and Abednego, that you refuse to serve my gods or to worship the gold statue I have set up? I will give you one more chance. If you bow down and worship the statue I have made when you hear the sound of the musical instruments, all will be well. But if you refuse, you will be thrown immediately into the blazing furnace. What god will be able to rescue you from my power then?"

Shadrach, Meshach, and Abednego replied, "O Nebuchadnezzar, we do not need to defend ourselves before you. If we are thrown into the blazing furnace, the God whom we serve is able to save us. He will rescue us from your power, Your Majesty. But even if he doesn't, Your

Majesty can be sure that we will never serve your gods or worship the gold statue you have set up."

Nebuchadnezzar was so furious with Shadrach, Meshach, and Abednego that his face became distorted with rage. He commanded that the furnace be heated seven times hotter than usual. Then he ordered some of the strongest men of his army to bind Shadrach, Meshach, and Abednego and throw them into the blazing furnace. So they tied them up and threw them into the furnace, fully clothed. And because the king, in his anger, had demanded such a hot fire in the furnace, the flames leaped out and killed the soldiers as they threw the three men in! So Shadrach, Meshach, and Abednego, securely tied, fell down into the roaring flames.
But suddenly, as he was watching, Nebuchadnezzar jumped up in amazement and exclaimed to his advisers, "Didn't we tie up three men and throw them into the furnace?"
"Yes," they said, "we did indeed, Your Majesty."

"Look!" Nebuchadnezzar shouted. "I see four men, unbound, walking around in the fire. They aren't even hurt by the flames! And the fourth looks like a divine being!"

Then Nebuchadnezzar came as close as he could to the door of the flaming furnace and shouted: "Shadrach, Meshach, and Abednego, servants of the Most High God, come out! Come here!" So Shadrach, Meshach, and Abednego stepped out of the fire. Then the princes, prefects, governors, and advisers crowded around them and saw that the fire had not touched them. Not a hair on their heads was singed, and their clothing was not scorched. They didn't even smell of smoke!

Then Nebuchadnezzar said, "Praise to the God of Shadrach, Meshach, and Abednego! He sent his angel to rescue his servants who trusted in him. They defied the king's command and were willing to die rather than serve or worship any god except their own God. Therefore, I make this decree: If any people, whatever their race or nation or language, speak a word against the God of Shadrach, Meshach, and Abednego, they will be torn limb from limb, and their houses will be crushed into heaps of rubble. There is no other god who can rescue like this!" Then the king promoted Shadrach, Meshach, and Abednego to even higher positions in the province of Babylon. Daniel 3 (NLT)

Do you hear the music? Can you feel the pressure? Do you feel your knees start to buckle as you realize that you are the only one standing, while those around you—even fellow believers, cower before a meaningless formation? May our God of the ages strengthen us and teach us as we study His Word more deeply.

What command did the King give to all the people?
_____
_____
_____

What was the punishment for disobedience? _____
_____
_____
_____

How did Shadrach, Meshach and Abednego respond to the most powerful King in the world? _____
_____
_____
_____

How did they respond after He gave them a second chance?

_____
_____
_____

Did the three young men fully expect God to rescue them?

_____
_____
_____

I find it very inspiring that their confidence lay in the fact that He *was able* to rescue them, yet they surrendered to the fact that they may die in agony anyway. They refused to dishonor the Lord by following the crowd or cowering in fear.

List the miracles that God did as a result of their bold obedience: _____
_____
_____
_____

What about you? Is God calling you to stand for something? Very little has changed in this world since those young men respectfully stood their ground for God. Our clothes may be different, but we still face pressure to reject God on a daily basis. What encouragement have you personally received from this amazing story? _____
_____
_____
_____
_____

Talk to God about your life and how He is using you to make a difference.

May He give you the strength to honor Him with all that you are for the rest of your life. May your testing in these years be a solid foundation for your future.

Real Wisdom from Real Women

"Not enough of my generation was equipped spiritually to handle all the changes in my lifetime. If you young people seek the Lord, you will know that your worth comes from knowing how much God values you. Then you will have the confidence to stand up for what is right. Someone once said, 'All it takes for evil to prevail in the world is for good men to remain silent.' Knowing who you are as a child of God will give you the courage to change the history of our country—in your home, school and community. "I can do all things through Christ who gives me strength." Philippians 4:13—Jeanne (my wise mother)

"Every man gives his life for what he believes and every woman gives her life for what she believes. Sometimes people believe in little or nothing and yet they give their life to that little or nothing. One life is all we have. We live it and it's gone, but to live without belief is more terrible than dying—even more terrible than dying young." —Joan of Arc, as she was being burned at the stake

Overflowing
2 Timothy 3:10-14
Matthew 5:10-12
Romans 1:16-17
Proverbs 29:25

Lord Jesus, help me to know You in a way I have never known You before. I need You. Amen.

The Great Physician

Who can make a hardened criminal a loving servant? Who can give sight to the blind? How can a victim become victorious? Who can be a Father to the fatherless? How can a mentally ill person be given a holy purpose? Who can give an orphan hope and a future? Who provides for the poor, single parent family? The answer is always the same: Jesus. All of the above are found in scripture, but they are also found in living examples around us today.

I am reminded of a young woman I met on a mission team a few years ago. She had been abused repeatedly by her grandfather who lived with them. She tearfully relayed stories of how he had lied to her, threatened her and took advantage of her since she was very young. Her story literally made me sick to my stomach. Some very logical questions raced through my mind: how can she ever trust a man in her life if her own *grandfather* hurt her so? How will she ever get over the emotional pain? She continued to speak and what began as a horrific story, ended in a beautiful testimony. She glowed as she told me how she found healing in Jesus and how He gave her strength to talk to her mother and get help. No one would ever count this young woman a victim, because she is no longer. She had turned her pain, bitterness, mistrust and despair over to Jesus and *she let Him be* her Savior. She is victorious because of Jesus.

I can give you countless examples of people living today that suffered from addictions, rejection, abuse, unhealthy relationships, shameful pasts, you name it—whose lives have been transformed. This is because they completely surrendered everything to Jesus.

As I prayed for you this morning, God revealed to me that so many of you have been hurt badly. I type with tears in my eyes for the pain that you have suffered in your life. You do not have to count yourself among the victims or statistics of whatever category of hurt you may fall in. There is not only hope, there is a fresh beginning and a glorious ending for you. An answer was given for you before you were ever born. Do you know that Jesus came *for you*? He went through indescribable pain, because He didn't want you to even have to try to carry the hurt alone. He suffered and died because He *wanted* to and He rose because of His power. He loves you too much to leave you without a hope.

Whatever hurt you are dealing with, He invites you to give it to Him. Here is a prayer to get you started. Continue to pray out loud or journal whatever you personally need to surrender so that He can be Lord of your life:

Lord Jesus, thank You for being the Great Physician. I believe that only You have the power to heal my heart and take away the pain. Lord Jesus, I know that You already know the pain that I have faced. If I am in an unhealthy situation, show me a way out and give me the strength to follow You. God, as I have been hurt, I know that You desire me to forgive those at fault. I realize that forgiving them does not make what they did right. Lord, I submit my feelings of anger and bitterness to You. Help me to take captive any thoughts that would dishonor You, loving Savior. Set me free from hatred and resentment and make me a new creation.

Thirsty?

Therefore, if anyone is in Christ, he is a new creation; the old has gone, the new has come! 2 Corinthians 5:17

The God of peace will soon crush Satan under your feet. Romans 16:20

For the Lord your God is a merciful God; He will not abandon...you. Deuteronomy 4:31

I pray that you will begin to understand the incredible greatness of his power for us who believe Him. This is the same mighty power that raised Christ from the dead and seated him in the place of honor at God's right hand in the heavenly realms. Ephesians 1:19-20 (NLT)

Challenge: Memorize these verses. Copy them on cards, paste them in your room, on your mirror, your space at school, wherever you can to surround yourself with assurance that you have been given victory because of Jesus.

In your journal...Copy *Psalm 147:3*: *He heals the broken hearted, binding up their wounds.*

Recopy it, but this time personalize it and pray it. For example, "Lord, only You can heal my heart and keep me from past hurts..." Write to God inspired by that verse.

_____
_____
_____
_____
_____
_____
_____

Real Wisdom from Real Women

"For anyone who has been sexually, mentally, physically, or verbally abused it is difficult not to go back to those times and dwell on them. I found that every time I visited those hurts buried deep within me, it only made me miserable, extremely depressed, and left me wallowing in self-pity. It was like hitting the tape recorder play button, then rewind button, then play, rewind, play, etc. I was the only one revisiting that painful part of my life; I was the only one suffering. My abuser wasn't suffering. It was in the past, why would he be troubled over something that he delighted in? I finally said **no**—to living with the hurts of the past, the hurts inflicted on me by others who didn't have a clue as to how much they hurt me and how much damage they did to my life. I bowed my head and asked God to take it from me. Do you know what He did for me? He directed me to a sheet of paper and a pen, and then asked me to write a letter to my abuser telling him how much he ruined my life, how much I suffered mentally and physically because of his abuse, and then He wanted me to tell *him* how sorry I felt for him and that I forgave *him*. I thought it was a joke. Why should *I* be the one forgiving and letting go? Didn't God understand what happened to me? It was no joke. And yes, God did truly understand what happened to me because He was there with me through it all. He never left me because His Word is truth . . . 'I will never leave you nor forsake you.' (Joshua 1:5). 'I am with you always . . .' (Matthew 28: 20).

After I had written the letter, I placed it at the foot of the cross of Jesus where it belonged because, after all, He suffered for it. My hurt and pain and abuse were nailed to the cross with Him, for Him to carry, and for me to let go of. He took the tape recorder and recorded over my hurt with His story......His depth of love for me that will never stop no matter what I go through, His dying on the cross and rising that I might live with Him each and every day with full confidence that one day I'll be dancing with joy in heaven.

Let go of the past because you are the only one being hurt by it. Put it on the cross where it belongs. Jesus died for it. It's not yours anymore."   -Anonymous

Overflowing
Psalm 57:1-3
Psalm 34
Psalm 28:1-2, 6-7

God, You have created me to worship You and serve You in a way that is unique to me. Unlock whatever holds me back and lead me there. I hold tightly to Your hand. Amen.

Free to Be

My faith really took off after I returned from my first mission trip to Nicaragua. I was committed to seeking God and I felt so free because I was learning (I still am learning, this principle by the way...) that only God's voice matters. I was immersed in His Word and spilling over with joy. I knew He was challenging me to find joy in Him alone. At that time in my high school, the big pastime was drinking. Alcohol was the source for shy girls or guys to feel confident or social. It was a vehicle for letting loose. It was contrived fun. God reminded me that He could give me more in Him. He showed me that I could have so much fun and pee-in-your-pants laughter without resorting to the keg in the cornfields. Life with God made drinking and purposeless pastimes seem about as exciting as unloading the dishwasher. Funny how God blesses us in ways we aren't even aware of. On several occasions, people would actually ask me if I was drunk at school or different events. (This still happens, by the way.) Sometimes that would open the door to a way to lovingly explain that God is my source of joy. I had many one-on-one talks with friends who wanted true joy.

Are you set free? I mean, *really* set free? Let's take a look at Psalm 63 to see how we get there.

Thirsty?

O God, you are my God; I earnestly search for you. My soul thirsts for you in this dry and weary land where there is no water. (v. 1-2)

I have seen you in your sanctuary and gazed upon your power and glory. Your unfailing love is better to me than life itself, how I praise you! (v. 3)

I will honor you as long as I live, lifting up my hands to you in prayer. You satisfy me more than the richest of foods. I will praise you with songs of joy. (v. 4-5)

I lie awake thinking of you, meditating on you through the night. I think how much you have helped me; I sing for joy in the shadow of your protecting wings. (v. 6-7)

I follow close behind you; your strong right hand holds me securely. But those plotting to destroy me will come to ruin. They will go down into the depths of the earth. They will die by the sword and become the food of jackals. (v. 9-10)

But the King will rejoice in God. All who trust in Him will praise Him, while liars will be silenced. (v. 11)

Write your thoughts about this Psalm: _____
_____
_____
_____
_____
_____
_____
_____

What does a life free in Jesus look like? _____

What does King David's longing for God cause him to do?
_____

After David has experienced God's presence, (in His sanctuary, v. 3), what does he say about God's love?
_____

Now, because he feels this way, how does he show his devotion to God? List as many as you find in verses 4-7
_____
_____
_____

How does David follow God? _____
_____

How much room does that leave for the opinions and lifestyles of other people? _____

What is God's promise to us as we follow Him closely?
_____
_____
_____
_____

Finally, what is the attitude behind verse 11? I see a lot of pride—good pride. Do you know that God gives us permission to boast about one thing in all of scripture? It is actually the only thing we have to boast about—that He, Jesus Christ, is our God.

You see, we are not called to point fingers and condemn the ways of others. We are called to know God. He will give us the right time to speak truth and to embrace the hurting or answer questions for the curious. We can go about our days with a loving resilience to people of this world. We love them, but we don't follow them. We love them, because we serve a God of love.

Ask God to help you follow Him more closely.

What people or behaviors will you leave behind?
_____
_____
_____
_____

What actions in the Psalm do you want to make a habit of in order to walk with God? _____
_____
_____
_____

Challenge: Memorize a section of the Psalm today. Keep those words in mind as you interact with others and go about your day. Reflect on them before you go to bed and talk to Him about your day.

Real Wisdom from Real Women
"If you're grateful to the Lord—for the big and small things, His joy just comes over you and you can't hold it in. It's an ever-flowing river. You are free to laugh and love. I can't explain it. God is just so good."—Aunt Reta

Overflowing
Galatians 1:10
Acts 2

Lord Jesus, open my heart to Your compassion and Your healing power. Amen.

Death Trap

~~~~

Consider all of these scenarios. Keep in mind: they are real events; real people.

A girl loses her father when she is in Kindergarten. The loss places a tremendous stress on her mother and younger siblings and as the years pass, they fall into despair and choose destructive lifestyles. Each of the three children was sexually active in high school. Only one out of three finished high school and none of them have a regular church home. It would be an understatement to say that their family and their lives have fallen apart.

A family of five tragically becomes a family of four as the father is diagnosed with cancer six months before dying and leaving his wife and three sons under the age of 13. The loss places tremendous stress on the family, but they fall in the direction of Jesus. They become more active at church and friends and relatives reach out in support. The mother "glows God" and all of her sons are extremely successful in high school, college and career. Just seven years after the death of their father they are closer to Jesus than they were before their father died.

A mother learns that her once darling baby boy is now a grown criminal and Satanist. He chooses to end his life in a slow and painful suicide—a sacrifice to Beelzebub. She is in utter despair before God. She meditates on God's character and faithfulness. She has no answers for her son's tragedy, but trusts in her merciful God for strength. She is a powerful speaker, author, prayer warrior and mentor to me.

My friends, this is an ugly world. We are children of the Most High holy God, yet we see examples of an unfair, unjust, cruel reality. Perhaps you have experienced the death of someone close to you and the sting is almost more than you can bear. You may have the comfort and assurance that your loved one is in heaven. You may not. You may scream at God and go through seemingly hell on earth to try to make sense of the situation. You may retreat from God's loving presence and let the cruel world harden you, or you may go through every conceivable stage of grief in the presence of your loving Savior.

Take a look at the examples. All events are tragic. We do not need to rank tragedies. They all hurt. The difference in the lives of each of these people is where they chose to fall when tragedy came to them. Those who fell into the arms of God received healing. Those who ran from God's embrace never healed. Sometimes, we see tragedy as a license to act out any sinful desire or rebellion that Satan would have us entertain. It may be a normal response to grief in the eyes of the world, but what you have inherited as a daughter of the King is not commonplace. You have access to God's own glory and goodness—He shares all that He has with you. My friend, if you are in crisis, remember that you have access to the goodness of the Lord. Draw from it—run to it—fall in it. Dwell in the reservoir of God's unfailing, unending love and grace. But for your soul's sake, don't fall into the death trap.

You might feel like you are supposed to just get through it all. Please understand that "getting through" a tragedy puts the pressure on *your* shoulders. If you know Jesus and are truly relying on what He has for you, if you've told Him that it's too big, too difficult for you to do on your own and you have no other option than to let Him carry you, than you are already experiencing victory and healing. He *will* carry you and then teach you a new way to walk.

I encourage you to change the way you talk to God. Do not simply ask Him, "Why?" but instead focus your meditation on God's character. Then allow yourself the privilege of falling in His arms and experiencing Him for who He really is.

Thirsty?

The Lord is close to the broken-hearted; He rescues those who are crushed in spirit. The righteous face many troubles, but the Lord rescues them from each and every one. Psalm 34:18-19 (NLT)

I remember my affliction and my wandering, the bitterness and the gall. I well remember them, and my soul is downcast within me. Yet this I call to mind and therefore I have hope: Because of the Lord's great love we are not consumed, for His compassions never fail. They are new every morning; great is your faithfulness. I say to myself, "The Lord is my portion; therefore I will wait for Him." The Lord is good to those whose hope is in Him, to the one who seeks Him; it is good to wait quietly for the salvation of the Lord. Lamentations 3:19-26

Praise be to the God and Father of our Lord Jesus Christ. He is the source of every mercy and the God who comforts us. 2 Corinthians 1: 3-4

But as for me, I know that my Redeemer lives, and He will stand upon the earth at last. And after my body has decayed, yet in my body I will see God! I will see Him for myself. Yes, I will see Him with my own eyes. I am overwhelmed at the thought! Job 19:25-27 (NLT)

For you, O Lord, have delivered my soul from death, my eyes from tears, my feet from stumbling, that I may walk before the Lord in the land of the living. Psalm 116:8-9

I believed in you, so I said, "I am deeply troubled, Lord." In my anxiety I cried out to you, "These people are all liars!" What can I offer the Lord for all He has done for me? I will lift up the cup of salvation and praise the Lord's name for saving me. I will keep my promises to the Lord in the presence of all His people. The Lord cares deeply when his loved ones die. Psalm 116:10-15 (NLT)

Journal your pain to Jesus. Choose a verse above that speaks to you. Speak to Him about it and wait in His presence. Write how He blessed you through it. _____

_____
_____
_____
_____
_____
_____
_____
_____
_____
_____
_____
_____

Challenge: Every time the pain revisits you, repeat one of the above scriptures again and let our Lord remind you of His faithfulness. Don't let the world dictate how your life will be as a result of your pain—let Jesus do something beautiful with it. (See Isaiah 61:3)

Real Wisdom from Real Women

"At that time, I would never have thought of it this way, but the death of my father-in-law was a gift to our family. Because of his death, Jesus has touched my family." –Lynn

"While my parents were Christians, they were not 'active' in their faith. As I was growing up, I didn't get a regular 'feeding' of God's Word. When I began my teen years, I had nothing to anchor on to, no place that I could come back to when I was in the midst of the many storms that I endured during those years. Too often I felt battered and bruised; afraid that I would drown in my own self-pity and despair. I'm not being melodramatic. This is how I felt. I can't tell you how often I thought about dying. I'm ashamed to say that I even tried twice to take my own life, that is how lost I was. During a particularly stormy period in my life, I clung to the book of James. I clung to it with my very life. *'My brethren, count it all joy when you fall into various trials, knowing that the testing of your faith produces patience.'* (James 1:1). Oh how I wish I had known that as a young woman. Now I am no longer afraid to tell young women to read His precious Word because there is life in these words and it is something no one can take away from you…ever! So what did I know back then? Well, remember when I told you that I had tried to kill myself? I found out the hard way that it wasn't the answer. The summer before my senior year of high school, my family was on vacation for two weeks. When we returned, I read an article in the local paper which changed my life forever. A good friend of mine had died the week before. I went over to his home, not sure what to say. His mom, God love her, greeted me and welcomed me into her home. She must have known how confused and upset I was and hugged me. Then, with what could only be God's courage, she told me that he had hung himself because his girlfriend had broken up with him. I was devastated! I was in shock! Here was my friend, good looking, a great student, star football player, popular ... and he killed himself over a girl. At that moment my life was changed forever. I thought about what kind of impact I would have had on those people in my life who loved me. I realized that NOTHING was worth taking my life for. At that moment I knew the world was not black and white but that 256 shades of gray were in between. In that realization, while I didn't know it at the time, God rescued me with that pain. He put His arms around me and let me know how precious I was, that each one of us is worthy because He loves us...even unto death on a cross." —Lori

Overflowing
Psalm 25
Psalm 34
Isaiah 61:1-3
Read 1 Corinthians 13. [Substitute "Jesus" for love.]
John 11 [Note Mary and Martha's expressions of grief
         toward Jesus and His compassion in their pain.]

Lord God, You hold all things in the palm of Your hand. I release my cares to You. Amen.

Drop the Rocks

Every morning when I rise to pray, it is as if I am strumming a harp in the heavens and sitting on a cloud…just kidding. A very frequent bad habit that I fall into is when I finally sit down to pray, my mind spins and rather than peacefully presenting my worries to Him and enjoying His presence, I nurse them in my own mind. To be quite honest, it is easy for all of us to be distracted by life. A dear professor of mine, Dr. Bill Cullen says, "If your mind starts to wander while you pray, pray about what's on your mind." It is possible to waste so much time *thinking* about our prayer requests and trying to fix our situation, rather than letting God have control. It's as if we are holding rocks—some jagged, some heavy, and some tiny pebbles that annoy us. We stare at them, talk about them, re-distribute the weight and clutch them as if the tighter we hold them, the better we can handle them. There's only one problem: clutching rocks does not make them go away. One thing that has helped me immensely is to start with a little meditation. It's something that Richard Foster writes about in <u>A Celebration of Discipline.</u>

Put your palms down in front of you. Ask God to take whatever is bothering or burdening you. For example, a rock you may be carrying is the burden of what path you are to take for the future. That can be a rock that God wants to take so that He can do something amazing in your life. Turn your palms over as if to drop that rock and every rock that you are carrying.

Once you have poured out your heart to Him, receive what He promises to give you. Turn your palms up and receive the promises He gives you in His Word. You may quote scripture or whatever He promises to give that you need.

Let's take a few minutes to go to Him this way.

Have you identified your rocks? What are they? _____
_____
_____
_____

Turn your palms over so that you are unable to carry them. Talk to God about what you have just given to Him.

Now turn your palms up facing heaven and receive His perfect peace, power, grace and love. Ask Him for spiritual blessings that He longs to give you.

You may say something like...

Lord, You promise peace that goes beyond my mind's understanding; a peace that this world cannot give. I receive it from You as a gift. Rain down showers of blessing on me today so that I may walk in Your favor, Lord Jesus, as You have created me to. Help me to keep looking up to You that I may not be tempted to bend and pick up the burdens (rocks) I have dropped at Your feet. I give all of my worries and problems to You. Take them and do something wonderful with them. If I need to act, move me to be obedient. If I need to be silent and wait, help me to have patience and know without a doubt that You are in control. I trust that You will, Lord Jesus. Amen.

Challenge: Do not take back a rock that you have given to God. He can handle them much better than we can! Read the following scriptures. Identify one or two that speak to you personally. As you are tempted to pick up a rock, pray the scripture and remember the promise in it that He gives specially to you today. May these words of life be all you carry with you:

Thirsty?

Give your burdens to the Lord, and He will take care of you. He will not permit the godly to slip and fall. Psalm 55:22 (NLT)

And God will generously provide all you need. Then you will always have everything you need and plenty left over to share with others. 2 Corinthians 9:8 (NLT)

As we know Jesus better, His divine power gives us everything we need for living a godly life. He has called us to receive His own glory and goodness! 2 Peter 1:3 (NLT)

Whether you turn to the right or to the left, your ears will hear a voice behind you, saying, "This is the way; walk in it." Isaiah 30:21

[Paul's words] And that is why I am suffering here in prison. But I am not ashamed of it, for I know the one in whom I trust, and I am sure that He is able to guard what I have entrusted to Him until the day of His return. 2 Timothy 1:12 (NLT)

Therefore, since we are surrounded by such a huge crowd of witnesses to the life of faith, let us strip off every weight that slows us down, especially the sin that so easily hinders our progress. And let us run with endurance the race that God has set before us. Hebrews 12:1 (NLT)

Can anything ever separate us from Christ's love? Does it mean He no longer loves us if we have trouble or calamity, or are persecuted, or are hungry or cold or in danger or threatened with death? No, despite all these things, overwhelming victory is ours through Christ, who loved us.

And I am convinced that nothing can ever separate us from His love. Death can't, and life can't. The angels can't, and the demons can't. Our fears for today, our worries about tomorrow, and even the powers of hell can't keep God's love away. Whether we are high above the sky or in the deepest ocean, nothing in all creation will ever be able to separate us from the love of God that is revealed in Christ Jesus our Lord. Romans 8:35, 37-39 (NLT)

Whom have I in heaven but you? I desire you more than anything on earth. My health may fail, and my spirit may grow weak, but God remains the strength of my heart; He is mine forever. Psalm 73:25-26 (NLT)

Then Jesus said, "Come to me, all of you who are weary and carry heavy burdens, and I will give you rest. Take my yoke upon you. Let me teach you, because I am humble and gentle, and you will find rest for your souls. For my yoke fits perfectly, and the burden I give you is light." Matthew 11:28-30 (NLT)

Real Wisdom from Real Women

"I feel like I'm drowning. I either need someone to throw me a life preserver or push me under. Sometimes holding on to the life preserver is hard work. The beautiful thing is that Christ's loving arms sustain us." —Jessi

Overflowing
Proverbs 20:22
Psalm 46

Lord Jesus, set me apart for things that I cannot even imagine—for Your glory. Amen.

Set Apart

When you hear the word holy, what do you think of?

_____
_____
_____

There are some different perceptions of "holy". Check which matches your line of thinking.

- ❑ Weird, out of touch; socially inept
- ❑ One who believes without a doubt that Jesus paid for all of their sins—sins committed and not yet committed.
- ❑ A nervous rule-keeper.
- ❑ Arrogant, too good for regular people
- ❑ Full of God's Spirit by the power of prayer and daily Bible study
- ❑ Constantly being changed into the image of Jesus.

According to scripture, that is you and I, and all of the people who confess Jesus Christ as their Savior. He has paid for our sins by dying for us and continues to change us to be more like Him as we seek Him. Christ calls us to be set apart as holy, children of God. There is a problem, however. You have been stereotyped to be in a very unholy, stage of life. This is a time when you are expected to, by society's standards, experiment sexually, drink heavily, experiment with drugs, rebel against or at least act annoyed by your parents and desire to waste a lot of time and money on insignificant things. I don't buy it. It is a lie of the devil. Of course, this often happens, but it is not what the God of the Universe created you for. The fact that you are reading this book and seeking to know Jesus Christ more intimately sets you apart. The wonderful thing about walking with God is He is always seeking to take you to a deeper, more exciting level in your faith.

Whose expectations will you walk in? Societies or your Creator's?

Ask Him to take you to a deeper level spiritually. He longs to do this for you! You will be surprised at the changes you see in yourself as you seek Him and let His Word live in your heart. Doing the things that many people your age think is fun, will become about as exciting as matching socks because God will be giving you assignments and that will change the course of history—and eternity.

Scripture says, "...*we are God's fellow workers...*" (1 Corinthians 3:9). That means we work *with* the Most High God (!) to impact this earth. He changes us and then we love and bring others to Him in miraculous ways.

Don't hold back and don't let *anyone* stand in your way. You are a holy chick. You were made for much more.

Thirsty?

Drink up these promises and write to God about what He has for you as you keep yourself set apart for Him:

But you are not like that, for you are a chosen people. You are royal priests, a holy nation, God's very own possession. As a result, you can show others the goodness of God, for

He called you out of the darkness into his wonderful light.
1 Peter 2:9 (NLT)

_____
_____
_____
_____
_____
_____
_____
_____
_____

Real Wisdom from Real Women

"I've been struggling with a friendship. One of my best friends, actually. We have lots of fun together. But God has been whispering to my heart lately that some of our fun is not what He has in mind for me. So I feel this big tug-of-war between being friends and being holy. How can I be a good friend to her and still be set apart for God? I don't think God wants me to run for the hills because I am too 'holy' for our friendship. And I certainly don't want to!

Well, God doesn't hide His treasures of wisdom from His children. And because I know He adores me, I went to my Teacher this morning and asked Him about it. And my completely faithful Lord *immediately* unlocked one of His treasures for me on friendship. 'My child,' He gently spoke, 'I never said you should build your friendship on fun. My kind of friendship is built on love. Instead of focusing on how much fun you won't have by doing certain things with her, focus on loving her. Help her when she is busy. Talk to her again like you used to. Stop worrying about losing her friendship. Just *love* her and let Me work on your hearts and keep your friendship alive. And *I* will provide the fun.'"

Thank you, my Best Friend, for my best friend. And for setting me apart for Your fun." —anonymous

Overflowing
Proverbs 14:12
Philippians 3:17-20
Psalm 1

Lord, make changes in me for Your glory. Help me to be a shining example of You to all I meet. When others see me, I want them to see You. Amen.

What Are They Thinking?

Thirsty?

You have heard that the law of Moses says, "Do not commit adultery." But I say, anyone who even looks at a woman with lust in his eye has already committed adultery with her in his heart. So if your eye—even if it is your good eye—causes you to lust, gouge it out and throw it away. It is better for you to lose one part of your body than for your whole body to be thrown into hell. And if your hand—even if it is your stronger hand—causes you to sin, cut it off and throw it away. It is better for you to lose one part of your body than for your whole body to be thrown into hell. Matthew 5:27-28, 30 (NLT)

Never speak harshly to an older man, but appeal to him respectfully as though he were your own father. Talk to the younger men as you would to your own brothers. Treat the older women as you would your mother, and treat the younger women with all purity as your own sisters. I Timothy 5:1-2 (NLT) (Paul was writing to Timothy, a young missionary.)

In "You are Expected to Be Beautiful" we talked about what motivates us to dress or look the way we do. Is your answer the same as it was in that entry? I ask you again, what or

who motivates you to wear what you wear, to smell like you smell… _____
_____
_____
_____

Confession time for me…There was a time when I really cared about the impression I had on others. I liked to show my figure. When I got attention from guys it made me feel good. I just thought, "They think I'm pretty or cute or whatever." These were subtle thoughts that controlled how I acted or what I did. A loving, seasoned, Christian woman shared on a mission trip the same thing I just told you. She had recently asked her husband what guys really think when they see a bare tummy or a girl in tight clothes. His response shocked her, me, and every girl in the room: "They think about what she looks like naked." I have since asked my husband and he confirmed it. I don't understand the way men think or what their psyche is made of, but I do know this—they are visually stimulated. A man of integrity who loves God may notice, but will do His best to turn his head when he is tempted. We have power to either help them resist lustful thoughts or we can lead them into sin.

Once, I was in my office at church, talking with a man old enough to be my dad. The top two buttons of my blouse were open. Somehow the way I was leaning forward in my chair gave him a wide –open shot of my cleavage. I had no clue about this until he asked me to button it before we finished our conversation! I was so embarrassed I could have crawled out on my belly! After I had buttoned my blouse all the way up to the top and turned about 11 shades of red, I took time to consider what had happened. It was a humbling lesson that I need to be more careful about how I come across to others. I commend him for his courage to be honest. A cleavage shot for my eyes is no big deal, but it can be terribly distracting for a guy. Worse than that, it actually swings the sin door wide open for them. I never would have considered that he even battled lustful thoughts. He was a grandpa for crying out loud! The reality stung: even in my ignorance, I had caused him to sin. Proverbs 11:22 reads, *Like a gold ring in a pig's snout is a beautiful woman who shows no discretion.* Oink Oink.

When we cause a guy to lust, what are we causing him to do according to Matthew 6? _____
_____
_____
_____

Take a look at these thoughts from real Christian men:

"When I walk into a room and there are girls trying to dress sexy I do my best to think of them as 'sisters' in Christ, but it is very hard when they dress the way they do. I pray everyday for God to use me to the fullest and to help me fight off temptation that the Devil puts into my walkway. So I ask you this not just for me but for all Christian guys out there, help us not to commit adultery by not wearing the mini skirt or spaghetti strap shirt. I know that most Christian guys don't look at the outer appearance, but rather your spiritual appearance and morals. If you have to dress that way and show some skin to get a guy's attention or something, then trust me, you don't want anything to do with that guy."
—18yrs

"Sometimes when I see how girls dress to look older, it makes me wonder if they are members of the girl-scouts trying to earn some secret, puberty-merit-badge. In order to receive the badge, they have to successfully look at least 4 years older than they are and they have to attract the attention of guys, not with their intelligence - their humor -their personalities (you know, those things that guys actually care about), but with their bodies. The unfortunate part is that those who receive the merit-badge actually give up a lot more than they gain." —29 yrs

"Instead of trying to change men by complaining about them, please take a look at what you can control, the way you look. Clean up your own back yard and sow some seeds that would make it easier for men to be around you without seeing you as an object. You will reap a harvest of honesty based on your personality, not your bra size." —41 yrs

"Guys seem to want to look at a "slut" or a girl that dresses like a slut, but rarely date her." —anonymous

I am convinced that every one of us has tried to manipulate men by the way we dress whether consciously or subconsciously. We are all guilty. Take this time to confess and ask for a new heart.

Take a look at 1 Timothy 5:1-2 (on the first page of this section). How is it that we are to relate to others in the body of Christ?

Challenge: Throw away items that could cause your brother in Christ to stumble. Ask Jesus to make you aware of how you dress so that He may be glorified. There are a lot of Christian women who have not learned this. Your mother or other women you know and love may have told you that you look great in your teeny-weeny shirt or skirt. Let your Lord guide you on this issue, not other people's opinions. You may be called to confess (not preach) what you have discovered.

Be warned and encouraged: Other girls will watch to see how you dress and act around guys. What a great opportunity to bless younger girls with a fantastic example of a holy chick who isn't obsessed with guys thinking she is hot! You may be freeing them from feeling like they have to keep up with a certain look.

Real Wisdom from a Real MAN!!!
"You would think that of all the places a guy could go to get away from the 'skin display' of some girls, it would be in church. But NO - it's almost worse there! Being a pastor, I am absolutely surprised at what I see coming up to communion - sometimes I have to work extremely hard to keep my eyes focused on the face - only the face, only the face, only the face... I'm afraid the day will come when I'm trying so hard to look away that I'll accidentally drop the communion wafer right down some woman's cleavage like a slot machine." —Pastor Anonymous

Overflowing
Luke 21:33-36
Romans 13:14
1 Corinthians 6:12
2 Timothy 2:4
1 Peter 2:11

Great God, help me to really get it. I want to know Your grace. Amen.

A Story about Grace

A friend of mine is an elementary school teacher who loves Jesus and her students wholeheartedly. She tells a story about a special little girl in her class named, Grace. Ironically, Grace was not so graceful. She was somewhat awkward and struggled with many things. She was the type of child who stood out, causing frustration to others because things did not come easily for her. Grace was not well liked and was often embarrassed about herself—especially her awkwardness. One day, Grace broke a keepsake on my friend's desk. She burst into tears and trembled as she told her teacher what she did, knowing that she deserved to be scolded. I'm sure she was probably feeling more like a failure than ever before. The eyes of everyone in the classroom watched to see how the teacher would react to their exasperating classmate. My friend then shocked them all with her response. She took Grace in her arms and said, "Grace, don't you know that you mean more to me than that silly dish? I love you and I forgive you."

I can barely get through that story without tears, for so many reasons. The first is that I have felt like Grace before. The second is that, my friend's mercy is so beautiful and God-like. It does my heart good.

It would have been easy for her to say, "Grace, that's why we don't run in the classroom. See what happens? Now get the dustpan, and clean it up." I think that we are used to hearing the logical response in this world much more than we hear the merciful response.

The longer I'm in this sinful world, the more I crave to hear stories about God's grace. God's grace does not say, "What broken dish? You didn't do anything wrong!" His grace acknowledges the disaster and loves the culprit anyway. That is how our God operates. He knows the mess we're in. He takes us in His arms and says, "That's exactly why I came. Let me do what I do best." Then, He forgets about our sin and longs to bless us with His love.

> How do you respond when He pours grace on you?
> Do you return the embrace and thank Him for His mercy?
> Do you shy away and doubt that He really means it?
> Do you continue to walk around in the sharp, broken glass, ignoring the sin that kills and His grace that saves?
> Do you pay attention to the reaction of others and miss His outstretched arms?
> Do you look for mistakes in others to make yourself feel better?

Wherever you are, it is not too late to take a deep look into the eyes of Jesus and see that His compassion is real and His words are truth. Say a prayer that He will help you get a fresh look at grace through these scriptures:

Thirsty?

How great is the love the Father has lavished on us, that we should be called children of God! And that is what we are! I John 3:1a

So we praise God for the wonderful kindness He has poured out on us because we belong to His dearly loved Son. He is so rich in kindness that He purchased our freedom through the blood of His Son, and our sins are forgiven. He has showered His kindness on us, along with all wisdom and understanding. Ephesians 1:6-8 (NLT)

This is real love. It is not that we loved God, but that He loved us and sent His Son as a sacrifice to take away our sins. Dear friends, since God loved us that much, we surely ought to love each other. No one has ever seen God. But if we love each other, God lives in us, and His love has been brought to full expression through us. I John 4:10-12 (NLT)

So now there is no condemnation for those who belong to Christ Jesus. And because you belong to Him, the power of the life-giving Spirit has freed you from the power of sin that leads to death. The law of Moses was unable to save us because of the weakness of our sinful nature. So God did what the law could not do. He sent His own Son in a body like the bodies we sinners have. And in that body God declared an end to sin's control over us by giving His Son as a sacrifice for our sins. He did this so that the just requirement of the law would be fully satisfied for us, who no longer follow our sinful nature but instead follow the Spirit. Romans 8:1-4 (NLT)

What did He reveal to you as you meditated? _____
_____
_____
_____
_____
_____
_____
_____

The more we taste His grace, the more we are compelled to give grace to those around us. It is imperative that we have an active confession life in which we acknowledge our flaws and thus receive God's perfect love. That power which is at work in us is able to transform us into world-changers. It's easy to know right from wrong and point it out in others, but it's a whole other way of living to continually ask for God's mercy to be poured on us. When that happens, mercy naturally splashes onto those around us. We become freshly aware that we do not deserve God's mercy any more than someone else may deserve our own.

Challenge: Ask God to show you someone that He wants to love through you. Sometimes, He puts people in our lives that seem nearly impossible to love. The only way we have the power to love unconditionally like our God is when we yield to Him and meditate on what He's done for us. As this becomes a conscious habit, you will be amazed at His power at work in you!

Real Wisdom From Real Women

"When facing hard times such as moving in 8th grade, a few break-ups, sinning against others, self-doubt and family arguments, I often did not know where to turn and I felt hopeless and alone. My parents did what they could to help, but knowing more about God's grace in these situations would have been life-changing for me. I wish I would have known about God's unconditional love, His forgiveness and His hand that helps through the difficult times of life. Instead, I often knew about conditional love like being shown love more often when I displayed perfection or a great achievement. I thought mistakes and challenges in life meant guilt and failure and that having conflict with others resulted in permanent, broken relationships. Later in life, I learned about God's gift: Grace. It amazes me that God will provide ALL the grace I need to face any hard time. He just does. I now feel like God has me in His arms. It feels warm; rarely hopeless and alone." —Anonymous

Overflowing
Luke 7:36-48
Ephesians 4:32
Luke 6:32-42

Dear Jesus, what is my purpose? Channel all my energies, abilities and desires so that my life will point to You and Your purpose. Amen.

What for?

Have you heard people say,

"Basketball is my life."
"My goal in life is to make it through medical school."
"I am obsessed with my body."
"I want to have a job that makes lots of money."
"My boyfriend and I are best friends."

I suppose we could quietly and respectfully ask, "And then what?" or "Where does that take you?" after each of these statements. Yet, all eventually lead to a dead end and a very dull life on this earth.

For someone who is walking with Jesus, listening to His voice and knowing Him, life never gets boring. Suppose your statement is, "Jesus is my life." The "where does that take you" response could go on and on and on... .

Thirsty?
What does it look like for someone to be sincerely obsessed with Jesus? Let's read Psalm 63:1-9

¹ O God, you are my God;
  I earnestly search for you. My soul thirsts for you;
  my whole body longs for you in this parched and weary
  land where there is no water.
² I have seen you in your sanctuary
  and gazed upon your power and glory.
³ Your unfailing love is better to me than life itself;
  how I praise you!
⁴ I will honor you as long as I live,
  lifting up my hands to you in prayer.
⁵ You satisfy me more than the richest of foods.
  I will praise you with songs of joy.
⁶ I lie awake thinking of you,
  meditating on you through the night.
⁷ I think how much you have helped me;
  I sing for joy in the shadow of your protecting wings.
⁸ I follow close behind you;
  your strong right hand holds me securely.

How does David describe the following:

    His desire for God (vs1)? _____

    _____

    _____

    God's unfailing love (vs3)? _____

    _____

    _____

    How he honors and praises God? _____

    _____

    _____

    _____

What does David do throughout the night? _____
_____
_____

What is his security? _____
_____
_____

Rewrite this Psalm by filling in the blanks to fit how you see God...

¹ *O God, you are my* _____;
   I earnestly _____. *My soul thirsts for you;*
   my whole body longs for you in this _____
   _____.
² *I have seen you* _____
   and gazed upon your _____.
³ *Your unfailing love is better to me than* _____;
   how I praise you!
⁴ *I will honor you* _____,
   lifting up my _____.
⁵ *You satisfy me more than* _____.
   I will praise you with _____.
⁶ *I lie awake thinking of you, meditating on you through the night.*
⁷ *I think how much you have helped me when I was*
   _____;
   I sing for joy in _____
⁸ *I follow close behind you; your strong right hand* _____
   _____.

Real Wisdom from Real Women
"Christ can take an ordinary day and make it spectacular. I can be scrubbing the floor, changing a diaper or just going about the normal things of life. As my heart converses with Him, He challenges and encourages me. He floods my heart with laughter and joy and fills my life (which may seem insignificant to some) with purpose." —anonymous

Overflowing
Psalm 33
Hebrews 13:5-6
Isaiah 26:8-9
Psalm 119:10

Dear Jesus, teach me to live each day fully trusting in You and looking forward to the surprises of the future. Amen.

Thoughts on Today and Tomorrow

What thoughts or worries flood your mind regarding each of these areas in your daily life?

Body - _____

_____

Mind - _____

_____

Spirit - _____

_____

Social - _____

_____

When you think about your future, what stresses you out the most? _____

_____
_____
_____
_____
_____

I would bet these questions were pretty easy to answer. If you are anything like me, you have things that have always, and seemingly will always, stress you out – whether in your immediate or long term future.

As a contrast to that, enjoy reading what your Savior has to say to you about these very thoughts:

Thirsty?
"So I tell you, don't worry about everyday life—whether you have enough food, drink, and clothes. Doesn't life consist of more than food and clothing? Look at the birds. They don't need to plant or harvest or put food in barns because your heavenly Father feeds them. And you are far more valuable to him than they are. Can all your worries add a single moment to your life? Of course not.

"And why worry about your clothes? Look at the lilies and how they grow. They don't work or make their clothing, yet Solomon in all his glory was not dressed as beautifully as they are. And if God cares so wonderfully for flowers that are here today and gone tomorrow, won't He more surely care for you? You have so little faith!

"So don't worry about having enough food or drink or clothing. Why be like the pagans who are so deeply concerned about these things? Your heavenly Father already knows all your needs, and He will give you all you need from day to day if you live for him and make the Kingdom of God your primary concern.

"So don't worry about tomorrow, for tomorrow will bring its own worries. Today's trouble is enough for today."
Matthew 6:25-34 (NLT)

What reassuring thoughts did God bring to mind for you in this passage? Copy down the phrases you want to remember. _____
_____
_____
_____
_____

God tries to make it easy for us. The Bible actually tells us the kinds of things that should fill our minds:

Since you have been raised to new life with Christ, set your sights on the realities of heaven, where Christ sits at God's right hand in the place of honor and power. Let heaven fill your thoughts. Do not think only about things down here on earth. For you died when Christ died, and your real life is hidden with Christ in God. And when Christ, who is your real life, is revealed to the whole world, you will share in all his glory. Colossians 3:1-4 (NLT)

What thoughts are to fill our mind? _____
_____
_____
_____

What does that look like for you in your daily existence?
_____
_____
_____

I am continually amazed at how our Lord knows about all the junk that can rob us of joy even when we are completely blind to it. He wants to protect us from being hurt and distracted by things that will not last; things that look and feel fashionable and important at first glance but have no lasting value.

He is the God of true joy, peace and surprises. In contrast to the many things we get bent out of shape over, the only thing in this world that He is obsessed with is YOU. In fact, did you realize that He is actually preparing a mansion for you? That's right – a mansion just for you; filled to the brim with every eternal blessing and perk you can dream of that will never fade, spoil or rot. This mansion will last forever.

Challenge: As you are tempted to get hung up on pointless things, take the advice we find in Hebrews:

Let us fix our eyes on Jesus, the author and perfecter of our faith, who for the joy set before Him [that's us] endured the cross, scorning its shame, and sat down at the right hand of the throne of God. Consider Him who endured such opposition from sinful men, so that you will not grow weary and lose heart. Hebrews 12:2-3 (accent added)

And Philippians 4:8:

And now dear brothers and sisters… Fix your thoughts on what is true and honorable and right. Think about things that are pure and lovely and admirable. Think about things that are excellent and worthy of praise. (NLT)

Jot down some thoughts on how you might think differently about your future based on the Bible passages you just read. Think in terms of the major themes in your life:

School: _____
_____
_____

Friends: _____
_____
_____

Extra Curricular Commitments: _____
_____
_____

Dating: _____
_____
_____

Job / Money: _____
_____
_____

Family: _____
_____
_____

Faith: _____
_____
_____

Real Wisdom from Real Women

"For seventy-nine years the Lord Jesus Christ has been the only constant in my life. I cannot remember a time when I didn't know Him or did not pray. However, there have also been times when I let some careless coasting cool the fellowship and He has called me back to a deeper relationship with Him. I have re-consecrated my life to Him many times. His patience with and faithfulness to me are humbling and gratifying.

"My latest experience in being called back into deeper fellowship with Him is a result of that dreaded 'C' word.

Three months ago a routine mammogram revealed a suspicious lump. Two dreaded surgeries and countless tests kept me praying but also questioning. As I was mulling over the details one day, I felt the Lord asking me, 'Are you going to trust 'Me?' I replied, 'Yes, Lord, I am going to trust You.' In my spirit I heard Him say, 'Then quit your belly-aching.' Now I don't know if the Lord talks that way, but those words have given me a smile and a firmer resolve to trust Him. My cancer is aggressive and the chemotherapy starting within the week will also be aggressive. So many things have happened in my life that I have confessed as, 'Just one more opportunity to trust the Lord.' This will perhaps be my most challenging one since I live alone and am already handicapped.

"Other opportunities to trust were when my husband had three different major heart-related surgeries. Each time I spent the day of surgery in a closed room by myself with only my Bible. Each day I read the entire book of Psalms and so focused on the Lord and His Word. The incredible peace and trust in Him that I experienced is indescribable, especially since there was no human with me to give me encouragement. The Lord knows my needs and I can't praise Him enough for the abiding joy He gives! I do not want to live a single day without Him." —Marion

Overflowing
John 14:1-2; 16:22
1 Peter 1:3-4; 5:7
Colossians 3:1-10
Psalm 16:11
2 Corinthians 4:17-18

Bibliography

Foster, R., (1998), Celebration of Discipline, Harper SanFrancisco, New York

Thomas, A. (2006), Tender Mercy for a Mother's Soul, Tyndale House, Wheaton

Webster's Dictionary, (1993), New Revised and Expanded Edition, Landoll, Ashland

Where do I turn ...

An index of topics

~~~~

...when I want to share my faith?
- God's Perspective..81
- The Way 49
- Why Me?..59

...for deeper Bible teaching?
- Disrobe...75
- God's Perspective..81
- Impossible Task...63
- Nowhere He Won't Go....................................69
- Still Standing...153

...when I need forgiveness and grace?
- A Story about Grace......................................191
- God's Perspective..81
- Sorrow or Guilt 113
- The Perfect Dad 141
- Why Me?..59

...when I need hope and healing?
- Death Trap..................171
- Suffering ....
- The Great Physician..................159
- The Perfect Dad..................141

...to find my identity?
- A Seasoned Sister..................45
- Contentment..................55
- Dance Like No One is Watching..................33
- Free to Be..................165
- One Thing..................147
- Renewed Commitments, Renewed Strength..................123
- Still Standing..................153
- Submission..................
- Temptation..................117
- You are Expected to be Beautiful..................15

...to grow in purity?
- Disgusting and Unaware..................39
- Disrobe..................75
- Idols..................129
- Set Apart..................181
- Sex, Etc. Part One..................93
- Sex, Etc. Part Two..................97
- Sex, Etc. Part Three..................103
- Sex, Etc. Part Four..................109
- Sorrow or Guilt..................113
- Temptation..................117

...to discover my purpose?
- Impossible Task..................63
- Set Apart..................181
- Why Me?..................59

...to find security?
    Cravings 25
    Nowhere He Won't Go 69
    The Perfect Dad 141

...for a healthy self-image?
    Picture of a Woman of God 135
    Why Me? 59
    You are Expected to be Beautiful 15
    Younique 87

...to grow in spiritual disciplines?
    At His Feet 29
    Cravings 25
    Drop the Rocks 177
    Free to Be 165
    Meditation 21
    Submission ....

...to de-stress?
    At His Feet 29
    Drop the Rocks 177

...to worship?
    Dance Like No One is Watching 33
    Free to Be 165

...to find out what guys think?
    What Are They Thinking? 185